TRACING INFINITY

TRACING INFINITY

Bridging the Gap between Earth and Heaven

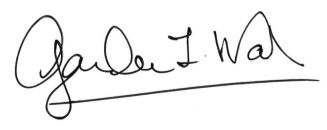

Best Wishes —

GORDON THOMAS WARD

ENGAGE
FAITH
P R E S S

Engage Faith Press
PO Box 2222
Poulsbo, WA 98370.

Published 2013 by Engage Faith Press

Printed in the United States of America

17 16 15 14 13   1 2 3 4

ISBN: 978-1-936672-47-9

Library of Congress Control Number: 2013941745

For Veronica, my angel

8i8

Contents

Acknowledgements xi
Foreword xiii
Introduction. xv

Chapter 1: Awake, My Soul, and with the Sun

A Winter's Walk with God 1
The Voice of God 4

Chapter 2: Wherever I May Wander

Schoodic Point. 9
Consolation on Marlboro Beach. 12
Sergeant Mountain. 15
Christening in the Cove. 18
Bobwhite 20
The Angel on Champlain 24
Memories in the Mist. 35
The Nine Faces of God. 38

Chapter 3: All Beautiful the March of Days

Initium Novum. 81
Perfect Fractures. 84
God's Transitions 86
Blooming for God. 88
The Unexpected 89

Wake Up!...91
Dog Daze..98
Raincoats...100
Samaritan Cardinals...............................105
The Garden Well...................................108
The Meadow of Heaven..............................110
Indian Summer.....................................114
True Nature.......................................116
Einstein's Oversight..............................119
The Instinctual Life..............................121
What's in a Name?.................................123
Harvest Home......................................126
The Child as Pilgrim..............................128
A Gift Outright...................................129
In Eclipse..132
Things We Get to Do...............................135
Snowsight...137
The Sounds, Sights, and Knowledge of Christmas....140
Backwards Vision..................................141
His Hands...143
Thank God!..146

Chapter 4: Abide with Me

Love with Patience................................149
Typographical Error...............................151
Proof...153
Dividing Walls....................................156
God of Child......................................158
Eulogy..161
Made New..165
Shutters..167
Beautiful Mess....................................170
The Persistence of God............................172
The Habit of Becoming.............................174

Out of the Deep. 176
River of Freedom 179
Moving at the Speed of God .187
Maximized Abilities. 189
Fix Me. 191
The Point of Departure 199
Gifting Divinity. 202
Useless!...Useful! 204
The String Bean Lesson 209
Learning to See 212

About the Author 215

Acknowledgements

Books such as this are not written in a vacuum, for there are always a number of people, from one's past and present, who provide invaluable influence and advice during the writing journey. I am indebted to all of the people in my life for their contributions and input.

Specifically, I would like to thank God for opening my eyes to infinite grace, Mike Anderson for his camaraderie and appreciation of the natural world in which we live, Joseph Bonk for his shared awareness of the environment, Jeri-Lynn Candage for her inspiration, my godparents Bill and Betty Feldmann for their spiritual guidance in shaping my concept of God when I was a boy, Fletcher Harper for his reflective words, Michelle McDaniel for her determined kindheartedness in Maine, Kelley McGlone Ramsey for sharing her experience with the whales, Rick Sweeney for his treasured friendship, Vince for his anecdotes, my parents Mildred and Warren Ward for their insights and my exposure to the natural world, Veronica Ward for her editorial assistance, and my dog Aztec for his instructional innocence.

Of course, I also want to thank my wife Veronica and my children Melina and Cory for their continual love, faith, and support, which mean more to me than they will ever know and is valued more than I will ever be able to express. You are all angels.

The author at Schoodic Point in Acadia National Park, Maine.

Foreword

"Earth's crammed with heaven,
And every common bush afire with God;
And only he who sees takes off his shoes,
The rest sit round and pluck blackberries."
~ Elizabeth Barrett Browning, "Aurora Leigh" ~

Gordon Ward has been paying attention. His book, Tracing Infinity, reveals that he has been watching the world with spiritual eyes. Ward sees evidence of God in everyday experiences. His stories indicate that he has perceptive antennae that find the Eternal in places that some might consider secular and mundane.

This book is crammed with heaven in the form of stories that stem from Gordon's extensive knowledge of botany and history and poetry. Here, God is seen in the first blush of puppy love, the branches of a dead tree, the adventures of Lewis and Clark, and the experiences of fatherhood. Ward tells us about times when he was enveloped by genuine warmth. This occurs because he has been able to see God in what might be described by some as coincidences. But he has developed the ability to see them as "GODincidences."

Much of this insight comes from the soul of one who is head over heels in love with God and life. "Believing is seeing" is a mantra that helps define his life and this book. He acknowledges his imperfections. But he is incredibly insightful when it comes to those things that only the soul can see clearly.

The reader will no doubt reflect on his or her own pilgrimage through life. The hope is that each will develop sharper vision for the God encounters that they may have missed in the past. It starts with each reader listing the ingredients in one's own life. Introspection is the first step. When we can see with spiritual eyes who we are and whose we are, we will be much better at seeing the burning bushes all around us. Then we move with the author beyond the walls of separation to a place where we allow our vision to help each other. This is what Gordon Ward has done for all of us in this book.

"What do you get to do today?" That might be the best result of a new view of the Infinite that Ward opens to us. We are indeed so much more than dust in the wind. We are all precious to God. Ward finds a way to express that without getting into divisive notions of exact definitions of God or religion. I think you will finish this book with more awareness of a life that is saturated with God. When it seems to be coincidental, that is just an example of God winking. Gordon Ward is indeed a spiritual being having a physical experience. He is as strong as a duck (you will get that later in the book) and as insightful as one on the mountaintop of faith. Join him on this pilgrimage of life and learn to trace the Infinite all around you.

Reverend Dr. Richard D. Sweeney
First Presbyterian Church of New Vernon
New Vernon, New Jersey

Introduction

*"We are not human beings having a spiritual experience;
we are spiritual beings having a human experience."*

~ Pierre Teilhard de Chardin ~

When my son was little, I used to watch him trace drawings from picture books. He'd lay the tracing paper over the image and very slowly follow the lines underneath his paper with his pencil. He'd never look too far ahead. Instead, he would concentrate only on the one or two inches in front of his pencil point. At times, he would find it hard to see the correct line to follow, and he'd have to lift the paper and peek at the image in order to find his way. In a short time, he was back to tracing and, eventually, found great joy in completing a drawing that resembled the original.

I think there are many similarities between this and the way we approach our lives. We live out our days tracing a path that was planned and chosen for us long before we had an awareness of ourselves, a path that exists in the midst of the infinite. We see only the events in the forefront of our lives, but we know they're part of a much bigger picture. Plus, the longer we live, the more we realize that our lives, our pictures, overlap those of others.

Sometimes it's really hard to see where our lives are leading. When it's hard to know what we should do, we peek under our life's tracing paper. For help, some of us turn to friends, some turn to life coaches, psychologists, ministers, or career advisors, and some of us turn to God. At times, we may be touched by a force that seems divine. Things occasionally happen that seem too amazing to have occurred by accident, and a solution to a way around the hurdles in our journeys becomes evident.

When we get our bearings and find our direction, we go on our way, following our life's path. With practice and experience, we can even get to a point where we glimpse the Divine in action all around us, wherever we may be. Our Creator, our God, the Life Force of all existence suddenly seems as close as our breath. I think we should seriously consider the Pierre Teilhard de Chardin quote, which suggests that we are *spiritual beings* having a *human experience*. I love that mind shift! I believe we are here to learn from our experiences while living as holy a life as we can; but, our Creator, much like any loving parent, is never far away from us, and when we learn our lessons in this world, we will transcend this earthly life.

This is not a religious book, yet it calls for readers to embrace their Creator. This is not a book that pressures readers to embrace any one God, yet it implores people to increase their awareness of a higher power at work in their lives. Most importantly, this is not a book about living a cloistered existence. It reminds people, engaged in the fullness of their lives, that they are never alone, that they can encounter the divine everywhere, and that every environment in which they may find themselves is holy ground.

This realization did not come in a flash of inspiration but rather as a kernel of thought that grew and took root over time. This very real, assured knowledge that we are defined by more than our bodies, that there is something greater than ourselves, that we are part of eternity and loved by a Creator that knows no limits, was impressed upon me during the course of my life to the point where I now consider it to be the basis for everything I do.

I have now given myself completely over to this Creative Force, but it has not been an easy road to the affirmation of my faith. My journey has been—and continues to be—filled with pitfalls, decisions, and events that are not in accordance with the guidelines I have set forth for myself or the ones established by my beliefs. I am broken and filled with flaws, yet I have come to a point where I accept them and look ahead.

God means many things to many people, and I would like to bypass, if we may, all the hurdles that separate one particular faith or denomination from another. Even if it's only for the time it takes to read this book, please try to suspend any limiting beliefs you may have, and try to think of God as a guiding life-force. This is the God to whom I would like to point in this book.

While my writing stems from Christian roots, experiences, and perspectives, it's only because that is where my background lies, and they are the teachings with which I am most familiar. However, I do not want to shut out any people of other faiths, as I know the experiences, messages, and teachings found within the pages of this book apply to anyone who walks this earth, regardless of creed, religion, denomination, faith...or lack of faith. After all, we are all God's children.

It's time to find and establish common ground, and it's time that we let the Eternal unify us. God is an abstract, often divisive, concept for many people, and I want to change that. The creative presence we call God is, I feel, very real and can be so for everyone. If nothing else, my life has taught me that, bit by bit. Along the pathways of my life, there have been times when the realm of God has left the spiritual door ajar and allowed the divine to present, and often thrust, itself into my world to the point where I could not deny it.

All of this took time, but the events about which I have written in this book have taught me valuable lessons that I feel compelled to share. I truly believe that our lives are saturated in God. Happiness and sorrow are constantly immersed in the Divine, and even at those moments when we feel most alone in the wildlands and winters of our lives, we are actually in the presence of our most trusted and dependable guides.

Many of my flashes of realization have occurred as a result of observing nature in many different environments. Meadows, mountains, gardens, coastlines, and open rangeland are all God's classrooms. All of these natural places offer a chance to be touched by flashes of inspiration because they are raw and unencumbered with the trappings of mankind and the distractions of everyday life. These wild places allow the subtle hints of divinity to present themselves in a more obvious manner. However, you can also find similar inspiration in your own backyard, on the street in front of your home, as a result of an event in your life, in a snowstorm, during an eclipse, or in the eyes of a child. If you expand your awareness and you look close enough, God will make Himself known anywhere you happen to be.

I believe that angels exist. I believe that our Creator dwells among us. I believe that if we are patient and remain aware, every one of us can begin to see how we spin out our earthly lives in accordance with the plan and guidance of the Eternal, in the midst of angels, and in our wonderful space of divine immersion.

We are all walking in the footsteps and in the presence of our God, fulfilling our roles in eternity, existing in the present and following our future in the same breath. We are realizing our life paths, which were laid out by our Creator before there was even anything in existence that any of us would come close to calling real.

When my children were young, they used to follow behind me, copying my movements, stepping up and down on curbing stones, skipping, walking, and running, shadowing my every movement. Like a child who follows a parent leading him or her on a journey, we do the same thing with our lives, only we are following a path forged by a timeless Creator who beckons us to follow. In a sense, we are all literally tracing infinity, and I invite you all to see how the Divine is touching all of our lives on our incredible journeys.

Gordon Thomas Ward
Pottersville, 2013

TRACING INFINITY

Chapter 1
Awake, My Soul, and with the Sun

A Winter's Walk with God

I don't remember what God said to me that night, but I understood His message. Neither do I recall God's image, but I knew His presence. We met on a walk of approximately 200 yards between my friend Richard Feldmann's home and my house in an area of Bernardsville, NJ, that is known as Somersetin. The year was 1969, and as a ten-year-old, the journey home was one I knew well. Most of the time I would travel either through the Feldmann's yard or along the Packard's driveway to a small, white garage. From there, I would cut across the Packard's hillside property to a break in a row of forsythia bushes. This opening allowed me to gain access to the westernmost corner of our property and walk across our yard to my back door. The route was short but surrounded the traveler with grass, trees, dense and often flowering shrubs, and a certain sense of independence and separation from the rest of the world.

On hot summer days, one had to be careful not to be stung by yellow jackets, which often nested in the grass. I learned this lesson the hard way by ignorantly walking through a myriad of these painful, little creations after they were distinctly perturbed by our neighbor's lawn mower, which had just passed over their nest. Swatting at my pants leg, which many of them had managed to enter, I ran jumping and yelling like a boy possessed all the way home, breaking speed records that I was later never able to replicate on the track.

In contrast, winter travels left their own unique impression. At times the snow was crusted enough to allow a boy of my former size to walk on top of the ice-capped snow without sinking through to the ground a foot or so beneath the surface. This slippery crossing along with the occasional, unexpected breakthrough added adventure and challenge to the journey. One journey in particular impressed me with one of the most poignant and peaceful epiphanies of my life.

Midwinter nights at Somersetin can be extremely crisp and frosty. On one such night I found myself bundled up against the cold and walking home by myself from the Feldmann's house after a night of sledding and hot chocolate with Rich. It was silent except for a frigid breeze that whistled across my face and the snow that squeaked and crunched under my feet as I walked. The sky, black and without a cloud, was a backdrop for a heavenly, stellar performance. Twinkling stars seemed scattered as so much glitter on a black velvet cloth, and a half moon, high in the sky, looked back at me and kept me company during the walk.

Without warning I felt a sudden compulsion to stop and raise my eyes to the sky. What was once a feeling of fortified resistance against the cold was replaced by an overwhelming perception of warmth that completely enveloped me, accompanied by a deeply comforting sense of peace and the firm knowledge that I was not alone in my life. I was taken by surprise and overwhelmed, transfixed and staring up into the face of heaven. The incident itself lasted for perhaps thirty seconds, but it impresses and affects me to this day. I don't remember the second half of the walk that night, nor do I recall arriving home. But I do remember, later that evening, looking out through my window at the night sky from underneath my covers, knowing that we are all loved and closer than we think to the Infinite. I had learned that when we unexpectedly break through the crust of life's journey, God is there to lift us up, and when we desire warmth in the long, dark periods of our lives, our Creator blankets us and wraps us in radiance.

Although I do not speak of it often, that evening during my tenth year has remained etched on my memory as the first time I felt a personal connection with something eternal and, I believe, a connection with God. The boy, who seconds before had been immersed in thoughts of speedy, Flexible Flyer sleds and mugs of hot chocolate, had undergone a profound change. Awareness is a spectacular gift for us all. I know I was not expecting or looking for anything or anyone in particular that frosty night, but something very precious had found me.

The Voice of God

Time to Leave

Early in her career, my mother, Mildred Ward, was a nurse at East Orange General Hospital in East Orange, NJ. Throughout my life, she has told me the story of how God spoke to her while she was at work in the early 1950s. No matter how many times she told the story, it never wavered, and her belief that it was God who spoke to her was sound and compelling.

My mother was agonizing over whether she should take a job in a dentist's office or stay on at the hospital. Both seemed to offer challenging career paths and promise for growth, so she was conflicted about which path to choose. Then, one afternoon while she was completing her chart, she heard a voice—a man's voice right beside her—speak to her. The voice said, "Leave. Leave now and don't come back."

My mother, startled, looked around her. No one was there… no loudspeaker, no patients, no nurses, no doctors. She was alone at the desk, save for the charge nurse who sat around the corner. The voice she had heard was distinct, and it was not in her head; it was like any other voice anyone might hear coming from a person with whom they were having a conversation.

Without hesitation, my mother packed up her things, and let the charge nurse know that she was leaving and not coming back. Now, in my mind, I would have expected some kind of surprised reaction from the charge nurse, some effort to make my mother stay, some questions as to her sudden decision, but this didn't occur. There were no questions, but there was support. The only words the charge nurse spoke to my mother in response were, "I understand completely. Good luck to you, Mildred."

Several weeks later, changes were implemented in the hospital, including the elimination of the very position my mother held.

My mother went on to begin a very successful and rewarding career as a dental assistant in Summit, NJ, and she never went back to East Orange General Hospital. My mother did as she was told. She put her trust in what God told her, and it worked out for the best.

Roadside Assistance

In the mid-1970s, my mother had returned to nursing in Overlook Hospital in Summit, NJ. She was a charge nurse on the night shift, so she would arrive home about eight o'clock in the morning.

On one particularly snowy night in January, my mother's shift had ended and her staff was preparing to leave. One of the nurses remembered that she had to buy groceries on the way home but had no money in her purse. My mother, learning of this, gave the nurse all of the money she had in her own wallet, so that the nurse could stop and buy the food for her family.

The snow was building up outside, so when my mother got on the road, she drove very slowly and cautiously on the slick roadway. As she traveled down the main road in New Providence, her car's engine began to sputter, and my mother looked down to see that she had run out of gas. She pulled over to the side of the road and wondered what she was going to do, a tinge of panic running through her. There she was, a woman with no money in the middle of a snowstorm at 7:30 in the morning in a car with no gas in a time long before cell phones.

Then she heard it: a man's voice broke the silence. It came from inside the car, yet there was no one in the car with her. The voice had very clear instructions for her. "Wait. When you see a red car approach, put your hand out the window, and you will receive help."

My mother waited several minutes, and a couple of cars did pass, but they were not red. Then she saw a red car in the side mirror. As the car approached her own, my mother put her hand out of the window. Sure enough, the red car pulled over in front of her, and a person she described as a "nice young man" got out of the car, came to her window, and asked if my mother needed assistance.

After my mother explained her situation, the man assured her not to worry. He proceeded to tell my mother to wait in her car while he drove to a local gas station for fuel, which he did. He purchased several gallons of gas, returned to my mother's car, and poured it into her tank. When my mother, wanting to reimburse him for the gasoline and his time, asked the man for an address where she could send a check, he said it wasn't necessary. He refused to be paid for the gas, and the only information he gave to her was that he was from a local church. "God bless you," my mother said to her angel in the snow. "God has blessed you, too," he said, and he returned to his car and drove off into the early morning snow.

The Given Name

When my son was still in utero, his mother and I, as most parents do, spent much time paging through books of baby names, agonizing over the absolutely perfect name for our son. We had many front-runners but no singular name that stood out from the rest. We presumed that we still had several months to finalize our choice, and, eventually, one of the books would offer up a name on which we could agree was the best fit.

One afternoon, while the house was quiet and I was writing in my home office, I heard my name called from head of the stairs. I got up and headed down the hallway sensing a hint of urgency in the voice. When I arrived at the foot of the stairs and looked up, there was my son's mom with her hands on her belly and standing at the top landing, having just awakened from a nap.

"I know the name of the baby," she said.

"What do you mean? Did you find one that you really like?" I replied.

"No. I was told what his name will be."

After a bit of a pause, I asked, "What are you talking about... 'you were told'?"

"I was in bed. I woke up from my nap, and I was just lying there, and I heard a man's voice next to me. It said, 'His name will be Cory, and he'll be beautiful.'"

Now, Cory was not one of the names we had been considering, but when I heard it, I fell in love with it immediately. Cory... Cory was it, and from that moment on, we knew what our son's name would be. We never questioned where the voice came from or whose voice it was that was heard. It might have been an angel, or it might have been God. All we knew was it was perfect.

When our son was born on October 9, 1996, we named him Cory Thomas Ward. And, yes, he is beautiful.

Chapter 2
Wherever I May Wander

Schoodic Point

I hadn't noticed what lay beneath my feet, really. At eight years of age, I was focused on the gargantuan sprays of surf that are thrown up on the large, flat rocks at Schoodic Point. Maine is famous for its rocky coastline, but at this place the rocky monolith drops into the sea with sheer cliffs meeting the dark, cold, surging, and unobstructed Atlantic Ocean. Those few hours leading up to high tide is the time when most people are encouraged to visit Schoodic if they want to see the sprays, for it is during this time that the water level is sufficiently high enough to create these amazing displays. Waves build in volume as they approach the shoreline, and at any given moment, hundreds of thousands of gallons of water and enormous amounts of energy are met by unyielding, vertical walls of granite and basalt. Left with nowhere to go, the water and energy are dispersed into the giant surf sprays for which this peninsula is known, photographed, and remembered. The amount of water thrown up in these jets of spray is dazzling, and, although the sets of waves can be seen breaking their way along the point, the displays can be very unpredictable.

While beautiful, there is danger lurking in the frothy jets, for the sprays have been known to sweep people off their feet and wash them off the cliffs, into the pounding sea, and to their deaths. When one gazes into the depths of the dark, rolling waters, it is frightening to think about what the last moments of life or consciousness must be like for those claimed by the Schoodic waves.

Hopping from one rocky ledge to another, most of my family members had dispersed out across the rocks, and I was making my way down to a point where I could get a better look at the majestic show down at the cliffs. Occasionally, I would stop to inspect a tide pool for barnacles, tiny shrimp, seaweeds, or an occasional sea urchin, but the sights and sounds of the surf would always interrupt and draw me to be nearer to the edge.

Now, it must be clearly stated and understood that I was not a thrill seeker. I had been warned by my parents of the dangers at the water's edge and told not to get too close. I had made up my mind to play it safe and stay what seemed to be a good distance away from the edges of the cliffs. Plus, I remained on dry rock—a good sign, or so I thought. My parents and my grandmother were watching and I felt safe. At one point, my mother decided to focus her camera on me in hopes of capturing me standing against a backdrop of a white plume of water. Looking through her viewfinder, she saw, instead, something terribly frightening.

At the very moment she framed me in her viewfinder, an unusually large and unexpected wave slammed into the cliff in front of me, sending up a fan of seawater higher and further up the rock than I have witnessed to this day. I had no time to react and nowhere to go for shelter. My mother saw the water raining down on me through her camera, and then I simply vanished with the salty foam. I saw it coming but only for a moment, and the next ten seconds were sheer terror followed by utter amazement. Before I had any time to react, I was pummeled and inundated with seawater.

The force of the water's impact knocked me off my feet, and all became grey. All I saw was bubbles, water, and flashes of light. Suddenly lying face down, I could feel myself being pulled by the undertow, and I was in a state of panic. Having been dragged closer to the edge, there was now a film of algae beneath me, which, combined with the smooth rock, offered me no traction and nothing to grab with my flailing legs, arms, feet, or hands that would arrest my slick slide. The reality flashed into my brain that I was being pulled toward the edge of the cliff where I would tumble nearly twenty feet into the rough sea. It was as if the ocean reached out with a monstrous hand and was intent on pulling me into her gaping mouth. The thought raced through my head that this is how I would die.

That's when I felt it. One hand grabbed the collar of my shirt, pulling me away from the cliff's edge while a second hand pressed down on my back. I stopped sliding, feeling like my shirt was caught on a coat hook, and I became aware of the remaining water racing over my shoulders, under the shirt on my belly, along my arms, and down the sides of my legs.

When the rush ended, and the water had drained away from me, the hands released me. I picked up my head, expecting to see my father, and looked around to see...no one. I was alone on the rocks coping with the fright of almost being washed to my death and simultaneously dumbfounded by the absence of anyone around me. Carefully and with considerable effort, I clawed my way up to a point past the green algae growth and got myself up on my feet. Stumbling toward my mother who was hastening to meet me, we embraced like no other time I can remember.

"Gordon, I thought I lost you," she said almost crying.

"Who stopped me?" I asked. "Someone stopped me!"

"I know, I know," she said.

When my mother had lost me in her camera's viewfinder, she looked up and saw me sliding. Then, she said, that the back collar of my shirt came up almost over my head, and I just stopped—only several feet from the edge.

"It was an angel," she exclaimed. "You were saved by your guardian angel."

After grateful hugs from my parents and a very relieved grandmother, we climbed into our station wagon. As my father backed the car out of the parking space, a tremble ran through my body, and I couldn't help but to stare at the edge. I stared at the spot down on the rocks, the place where I almost died—and the place where I was saved.

Consolation on Marlboro Beach

When I was fourteen years old, I fell in love for the first time in my life. Her name was Jeri-Lynn, and she lived very close to the place where my family vacationed every summer in Maine. Her parents and grandparents were friends with my parents, and when we met for the first time at a family gathering, it was magic. At that point in my life, I had never met any girl that made me feel as wonderful as Jeri-Lynn did. As a result, she and I spent nearly three weeks almost constantly in each other's company. We shared our first, real kiss together, and we fell in love.

It was a summer romance, to be sure. We both knew that I'd have to travel back to New Jersey when our family vacation was finished, but we tried to ignore that fact as much as we could. When the time finally came to say good-bye, we were crushed. I remember that afternoon being a blur. I couldn't stop thinking about her and about the year that would go by before I would see her again. Love had never hurt me before that moment, but as I sat on the back steps of our cottage, I felt that feeling, that heavy, yearning hurt, which most of us have come to know all too well in our lives. It wasn't the last time I would feel this overwhelming emotion, but it was definitely the first. I didn't know how to shake it, and I felt like a part of me was dying. Anyone with any experience in love will know that recovery from this emotion comes with time, but when it's a new feeling, you'll also remember that it hits you like the proverbial ton of bricks. And it lingers, emotionally oppressive and persistent, with no end in sight.

Trying to escape my parent's efforts to make me feel better and outrun my heart at the same time, I decided to go down to the beach where she and I once walked. I don't know if I was searching for solitude or making a vain attempt to bring memories of Jeri-Lynn to life, but I found myself sitting on a white boulder at the edge of the water on Raccoon Cove. Ghosts of Jeri-Lynn and I walking the beach were everywhere I looked. As I sat there, wishing that the pain in my heart would subside, I called out to God to make the feeling stop.

That's when it happened. Something astounding occurred at that moment. I had a feeling come over me that I had only experienced at one other time in my life, when I was ten years old. A sudden, genuine warmth enveloped me and stayed with me for about one minute. It actually permeated every fiber of my being. I felt as though someone was consoling me, and all of the pain that was in my heart vanished, drained from me as though it were washed out by the tide. Instantly, my mind was clear, and I felt free of the heavy love-sick emotion I had been carrying with me.

Standing up and looking around me, I half expected to see something or someone, anything that would account for this experience. Something this profound, I thought, must leave some trace in its wake. I never doubted what it was. There was something divine that touched me on that beach. Whether it was an angel or the peace of God, there was no one on this earth that could tell me otherwise. When this experience happens, it is so unique that it doesn't compare to anything else. If you've ever felt this—and I believe many of you have—you know exactly what I mean. One is left with a feeling of being washed clean and full of joy, and the world, which was moments before so dark, is unexpectedly bright and filled with promise and love.

If this story leaves you with a thought, let it be this. Don't ever think we are alone in this world. You may call it a guardian angel or the love of God, but there is a divinity that is with every one of us, every step of the way through our lives. At times it helps us without our awareness, but sometimes it hears our cries for help. Sometimes it knows our pain, and sometimes it simply sits down beside us, embraces us, and takes away our burdens.

Sergeant Mountain

I paused on my hike to raise the water to my lips. The heat of late morning had forced me to shed my long-sleeved shirt, and I had learned through experience the importance of staying hydrated when hiking, especially when one is on open rock, out of the shelter of the tree line. As I drank, the scent of my sunscreen mingled with the sea air and the primitive, earthy smells of the grasses and wild blueberry on the mountain's rocky flank. I had climbed this mountain several years before, and I knew the trail that lay before me. Looking up and sighting my intended route between the rock cairns, the sunbaked, bald, open summit looked familiar; yet for some reason the pink granite summit appeared almost timeless on that day, presenting itself like an ancient scene from a page out of a church text.

I was transported to a first century landscape, and the vista toward the summit of Sergeant Mountain became an ancient place of execution. People pushed and bustled around me, shouting and jeering. The mass of them moved the way a flock of birds fly—with a single mind and a solitary intention. In a flash, the crowd fell away, opened, peeled away like withered rose petals to reveal a man with long, matted hair, covered in dust, sweat, and dried blood. He had stumbled and fallen as a result of torture and the forced march toward His own death, His hands, knees, and feet on the ground, His ribcage heaving with utter exhaustion, sucking in air as quickly as He could, resembling a man at the end of a grueling race.

And then He turned His head toward me. In that moment, my senses zoomed, and His eyes became the world, and all I saw was peace and light, wonder and eternity. A vortex of all I knew and had yet to dream lay beneath and beyond His brow, lashes, and irises. His pupils were the doors to infinite love, compassion, grace, and wisdom. His eyes spoke, mouthing words that lips could never form as perfectly, and then, as suddenly as He appeared, He was gone from sight, dispersed into every particle of earth and sky around me. I was back on the mountain.

For a solitary moment, the summit marker resembled a cross on a hill, and it drew me up, higher and higher to 1,373 feet, my thirst had disappeared, and the world lay beneath me. I was in Acadia, and God was in the rocks. God's hands reached out in the butterflies and grasshoppers that flitted over the stony land. It was God's voice that resonated in the wind that swirled around the summit cairn, and as the Creator quivered with life, the land below me trembled with activity. And all the time, every second, there I was, cradled in the great forever. I felt like I was let in on a holy secret, and I wanted to shout out to the world and ask the question, "Can you see this, too? This energy, this surging current, can you feel this unimaginable, wondrous sense coursing through you?"

Of course, I didn't shout. I didn't even open my mouth to speak. I couldn't find the words to describe what it was I was feeling, although it was the most real my senses had ever been, and it was at once the most natural and aware state in which I had ever been suspended and immersed. I sat at the top of Sergeant Mountain in Acadia National Park with a thousand bells clanging in my chest—rung by a thousand angels—and I could hardly breathe, stunned by the beauty, while the hand of God unfurled everything in my sight, and I wanted to cry and sing and laugh all at once because I had just been shown, and I understood. For the first time in my life, I'd left remedial living at the door and surveyed the space before me. Pain and beauty, living and praying, dying and rejoicing in life are inseparable. None is better than the other.

In the past, I picked my bouquets of life like blooms for a vase. Fool! Shatter the vase and cast the bouquets out of doors. There are thousands of pieces of God lying in wait just outside my skin, awaiting the mind shift. They have always been there to see, but I needed to align my senses to the Infinite. This sacred ground, this *holy* land, it was battering my brain, endeavoring to impregnate my mind since I was born, and it finally broke through my perceived reality to fertilize my existence, and I am now transformed. It unveiled those two blind stones in my head to see; to see the wondrous garden, the sumptuous table spread before us, blessings too numerous to count in every second we live. It's simple, really. Thoreau and Emerson were on the right track and the apostle Thomas had it backwards. *Believing* is seeing. Everything is God, and we are all moving in the midst of the Creator, swallowed up, digesting in the bowels of creation, taking the ride of our lives, and all we have to do is see the Infinite within the infinitesimal and give thanks.

Christening in the Cove

Sometimes a moment unexpectedly grabs you by the throat and almost wills you to see the Divine in the world, no matter what is on your mind. Just such a moment happened to me in 1988 in Marlboro, Maine, and it moved me to write a poem, which I've included at the end of this essay.

It was July, and I was on vacation in a lovely, peaceful, summer house overlooking Raccoon Cove and Frenchman's Bay. My daughter, Melina, was thirteen months old, and on a spectacular, July day, I had it in my mind that I would like to christen her in the water that lapped at the shoreline below our cabin. The morning light glistened on the waters of the high tide, which had flooded the cove, and the stillness of the morning was broken only by the sounds of shorebirds, warblers, and the morning breeze in the branches of the shrubs that lined the edge of the hill overlooking the water.

Taking Melina in my arms, I strolled across the grass in front of the house and down the dusty driveway of rounded stones and pebbles. From there, I descended the grey, wooden stairs that penetrated the shoreline thicket and led to the water and one of those quintessential, Maine beaches strewn with rocks and shells. Melina seemed mesmerized by the water, and I chose a large, light-colored, conglomerate boulder to sit upon in a spot that allowed my feet to remain dry but also allowed me to reach the clear water.

I collected my thoughts. I told Melina that I had treasured memories of this beach from my own childhood, that it was a very special place for me because of the summers I spent there, but mostly because it was the place where I felt enveloped and consoled by the warmth of God when I was fourteen years old. For all of these reasons, I wanted to christen her on this rock. It's the place where I wanted the grace that I had experienced so many years before to now fall upon my daughter.

Holding her in my lap with my left arm, I put my right hand in the cove, scooped up three handfuls of the water, and spread them on the black hair of Melina's head, saying, "Melina Danielle Ward, child of the Covenant, I baptize you in the name of the Father, and of the Son, and of the Holy Spirit."

When I was finished, we just sat still. I was wrapped in the awe of the moment. We listened to a symphony of sea sounds. There were the continual sounds of water licking at the pebbles and the crackling sounds of tiny whelk and periwinkle shells being tossed in the small waves, and every so often, the music of the sea was punctuated by the calls of gulls and loons. I was lost...lost in the peace and the wonder and the honor and the sheer joy of that experience, but there was something else that stirred just underneath all of these sounds. Some may say it was just the breeze, but I heard a voice whispering to my daughter over and over saying, "I love you. You are mine. I love you. You are mine. I love you. You are mine."

Christening (for Melina)

When you were small and new to life, …my angel child,
I took you to the water's edge,
a place that knew me as a boy.
We stood among the shells and rocks
and gulls and turning tides and time.
Then, gathering you into my arms,
we sat upon a boulder seat
and gazed out on the morning sea.
I dipped my hand three times into
the salty water at our feet
and christened you on jet-black hair, …our angel child,
full of joy, enough, it seemed,
to make the tides and time stand still
while seabirds sang your praise in prayer
and empty, hollow shells that crackled
in the rhythmic, lapping waves
held not the sounds of surging sea
but God's voice whispering in our ears.

Bobwhite

In the summer of 2009, my son and I were on vacation in Marlboro on the coast of Maine. It was the same location where I christened my daughter in the cove twenty-one years earlier. The location of this particular house is, in my opinion, simply idyllic and is one of my favorite places on Earth. The only sounds one is apt to hear are the seabirds and the lapping waves. At night, the stars put on a show unrivaled by any other location I have been. A stillness envelopes the shoreline, making sleeping with an open window quite comforting, being lulled to sleep by the sounds of turning tides until night is chased away by the light of the coastal dawn.

On one of these mornings, as I was rousing from slumber, in that mysterious stage between sleep and consciousness, the thought "Bobwhite" suddenly made me open my eyes to awareness. As I lay quietly in bed, wondering why I woke with this on my mind, I heard the distinct call of this small, ground-dwelling bird, a species of quail whose full name is the Northern Bobwhite. The clear, distinctive, whistling call of these birds, "bob-WHITE" or "bob-bob-WHITE," is most recognizable. The syllables are slow and widely spaced, rising a full octave in pitch from beginning to end.

Now, I can't remember ever hearing this bird in the wild before this, so I was a little surprised to realize that I was actually identifying this bird solely from its call. Rising from bed and donning some clothes and a jacket, I crept past my son's room, ventured out on the deck, and looped around to the end of the house that faced a line of shrubs on the side of the yard.

Eventually, I heard it again, "bob-bob-WHITE," and I responded with my own whistled imitation, "bob-bob-WHITE." Amazingly, the bird, which was, up until this point, hidden in the branches, flew down to the ground where I spotted it walking out to the edge of the grass, apparently curious to find the source of my call. "This is amazing," I thought. "I wonder if it will keep talking to me." Again I whistled, "bob-bob-WHITE," and immediately the bird responded.

This was something Cory had to witness, so I tapped on his window, woke him up, and urged him to come outside. I dried a couple of chairs, which were still wet from the morning dew, and both of us settled down to communicate with the bird. We took turns, alternately whistling the call. Each time we whistled, this bird responded. It was a magical, almost spiritual experience! Here we were actually communicating with a Northern Bobwhite, a bird that doesn't occur naturally in that region, as the morning sun warmed and dried the world around us.

We had orange juice, fruit, toast, and tea on the deck, and after a good hour of dialogue with the bird, we decided to pack up for our day in the kayaks. Off we went with our gear, across the lawn and down the wooden steps to the beach. The last thing we did as we began our descent of the stairs was whistle, "bob-bob-WHITE." The reply, "bob-bob-WHITE," almost sounded like "have a good day."

Six hours later in mid-afternoon, Cory and I were in our kayaks and approaching the shoreline below our house, tired but fulfilled from our day on Frenchman's Bay. I thought it would be interesting to call out to our Bobwhite friend, just to see if he was still in the area and if he would respond to us. With more than a bit of doubt, we took turns whistling. After about five calls, we heard a response. Sure enough, as we climbed the stairs, we saw that our Bobwhite was still in the shrubs, and we spent the remainder of the day occasionally conversing with our feathered friend.

As evening drew upon us, I began to think about what it was that made me receptive to the Bobwhite's call. Was it because his call is so unlike the other birds that it stood out among the rest? Was it the proximity of the bird just outside my open window? Perhaps it was due to the fact that I was just rousing from sleep, and my mind was not cluttered and preoccupied with the thoughts of the day. Whatever it was, I heard the call and was drawn toward it, and it completely changed my day. My senses were much more attuned all day, and, as a result, the world split open at my feet. Sights and sounds, both diminutive and colossal, resonated within me in a new manner. I was open to sensing so much more because of the experience with the Bobwhite.

I began to think that this situation is similar to our response to God's voice. How does God call and speak to us? What voice does God use to call us? Surely, God speaks to us through His word, our thoughts, conversations with others, and other circumstances. The Bible recounts several incidents of God speaking to man in an actual, audible voice. In the book of Matthew, verses 3:13-17 and 17:1-17 describe a voice heard from heaven at the baptism and transfiguration of Jesus. Other times the "voice" is interpreted differently. In the book of John 12:27-30, it is said that Jesus was addressed by an angel and that a voice was heard, while others in the crowd said it was thunder. In Revelation 14:2, the voice of God is described as "like the sound of many waters and like the sound of loud thunder; the voice I heard was like the sound of harpists playing on their harps." Additionally, Ezekiel 10:5 indicates, "The sound of the wings of the cherubim was heard as far as the outer court, like the voice of God Almighty when He speaks." So, if the voice of God can sound like all these things, couldn't the voice of God also be heard in the call of a Bobwhite?

The voice of God comes for our sake—to spur us to action. We need to decide to act. We are often stymied in our lives by something I call the *Inertia of Inaction*. Do you know the Law of Inertia? It states that an object at rest tends to stay at rest and an object in motion tends to stay in motion with the same speed and in the same direction unless acted upon by an unbalanced force. Therefore, if we do the same thing, day after day, or, if we do not act, we will, in all likelihood reap the same results—the inertia of inaction. If you want a richer and fuller spiritual life, you have to first decide to be willing to search for it and be open to possibilities. You have to change the way you view the world in order to be open to the events that will change your course.

In first aid classes, instructors talk about the three Cs: Check, Call, Care. Ideally, they are accomplished in that order. Check the victim(s) and the scene, Call for help, and Care for the victim(s) until help arrives. However, all first aid instructors will tell you that the three Cs begins with a D because the very first step is actually Deciding to act. It's the same with faith and spirituality. Individuals need to decide to search out the divine in their lives and be open to those teaching moments in life where the divine manifests itself. In regard to this story, it was the call of the Bobwhite that opened my eyes, if you will, to the subtle and spectacular beauty that surrounded me. In many ways, that bird was God speaking to me and my son saying, "I am all around you. The divine surrounds you, engulfs you, and it can use any form to communicate with you. All that's needed is the willingness and the sensitivity and the awareness to listen closely."

What is God saying to us, and where are we being called? God speaks to everyone individually and calls us in many different directions. Listen…please…really listen! Let the waves and the force of God's voice move you to action, appreciation, and awareness! It may sound like thunder or harps. It may come through His word, our thoughts, our conversations with others, or other circumstances. It may sound like a spoken voice or wings of cherubim or many waters or maybe even a Bobwhite, but God's voice can be heard. Shhh! Listen! What is God saying to you?

The Angel on Champlain

In August of 2001, I flew by myself to Bangor, Maine to spend five days immersed in Acadia National Park, one of the most stunning and gorgeous locations I know on Earth. Being a mountain hiker, the jewel of this trip promised to be a day-long hike, during which I planned to summit six of the park's mountains: Champlain, Penobscot, Sergeant, North Bubble, South Bubble, and Pemetic.

Traveling lightly, I got off the plane, rented a small car, and headed for Acadia. I spent that first night in Bar Harbor, talking to some locals, checking the next day's weather, and poring over my trail map, making sure everything was in place for the hike. I couldn't wait to begin. I don't think I feel more alive at any other place in the world as I do on the summits of Acadia.

The next day dawned brightly, and I arrived at the Champlain Mountain trailhead early enough to minimize my exposure to the sun on this first ascent. I chose to climb the Precipice Trail, considered to be the most challenging and well known hiking trail in Acadia National Park with an exposed and almost vertical 1,000-foot climb up the east face of Champlain. The trail, according to the guide books, is only recommended for physically fit and experienced hikers who have no fear of heights. The Precipice parking area is at the base of the Precipice cliff on the east side of Mount Desert Island about 1 mile north of the Schooner Head entrance fee station on the Park Loop Road. The hiking trail has many rungs and ladders along the trail's length and is approximately 1.6 miles to the summit. When I arrived, Acadia had just lifted the trail restriction that protects the returning and endangered Peregrine falcons that nest on its cliffs.

Eager to begin, I hurriedly filled my pack, locked the car, and approached the trailhead. Before beginning the ascent, I noticed several people gathered around two park rangers and naturalists who were at the Precipice parking area, answering questions about the Peregrines, and allowing people to view the falcons through a telescope. I took a peek through their scope, talked with them a bit, and then headed up the trail. This was my second climb up the Precipice Trail, and it was everything I remembered: a thrilling climb with spectacular views of Frenchman's Bay, Schoodic Point, and the Atlantic Ocean.

Arriving at the top, I found a place to sit on the bald, pink granite summit, drank some water, and opened my pack to get a piece of gum. One could spend a great deal of time on the top because the views from this 1,058-foot summit are breathtaking, but I was there for more than just taking in the sights. I still had five mountains on my itinerary, all of which encircled Jordan Pond, and to reach them I had to get back down to the car and drive halfway across the island.

Zipping my pack closed, I made my way down the north trail, which is less steep and loops back around to the Precipice parking lot. I was making good time. When I reached the parking area, I hopped in the car and drove about thirty minutes to the Jordan Pond parking lot. During the shoreline drive above rocky cliffs and picturesque coves and beaches, I reviewed in my mind where I wanted to hike, hoping desperately that I would be able to snag a parking space at the Jordan Pond House, a restaurant that sits at the south shore of Jordan Pond and offers dramatic views of the North and South Bubbles, which rise from the opposite end of the pond. However, I knew the parking lot fills up early and quickly due to the restaurant, so I doubted I would find a space to park.

Sure enough, when I arrived, the lot was at capacity, but I did manage to get a close space in the overflow lot several hundred feet up the road. I locked the car, secured the keys in my pack, slung it over my shoulder, made my way around the Jordan Pond House, crossed the carriage trail, and approached the Penobscot Mountain trailhead.

Penobscot is also a mountain I had previously climbed. In fact, except for Pemetic, all of the mountains in my itinerary were familiar to me. This was good because I knew what to expect, and I knew my timing. I also knew that the trail up Penobscot was mostly over open rock, which would be hot, but I had plenty of water and a water purifying pump with me. Breaking out of the tree line and with the false summits of Penobscot looming before me, I made my way up the expanse of the mountain's flank. I stopped only briefly at the 1,094-foot summit, long enough to gaze down at Jordan pond to the east and take a few photos, and then set my sights on Sergeant Mountain.

Sergeant was going to be the tallest mountain on my circuit. At 1,373 feet in elevation, it is the second highest peak on Mt. Desert Island, exceeded only by Cadillac Mountain, which rises

157 feet higher. I was looking forward to the hike to Sergeant, because the trail from Penobscot to Sergeant winds down into a small col in which lies a small and remote body of water known as Sergeant Pond, which, incidentally, was the first pond to be formed in Maine when the ice shield retreated. It's secluded, great for swimming, and nothing sounded better on this ninety-degree day. A quick dip of my head, legs, and feet in Sergeant Pond and an opportunity to refill my water bottles were my rewards for the hike down Penobscot. Then it was upwards to the summit of Sergeant Mountain.

While every mountain has its own personality, Sergeant had a distinctly different feel than the other two mountains I had climbed that day. Its summit is visible long before you reach it, and it's more dome-like. I was again climbing up through trees and then onto open granite, but I felt more secluded. There were fewer hikers on Sergeant, and, once on top, the views are less obstructed, especially from north to south. Again, I didn't tarry long on the top, only long enough to have a light lunch consisting of an apple, energy bar, and a bag of nuts. My time was precious to me, and three mountains were still calling my name.

Down the east flank I went, crossed the carriage road, and wound my way around the north shore of Jordan Pond. The Bubbles, North and South, rise above this end of Jordan Pond and are very visible, so I got the chance to see them almost continuously during this section of my hike. Now, to be sure, these are not big mountains. The North Bubble has an elevation of 872 feet and South Bubble rises to 766 feet. Still, when climbed consecutively, the combined climbs are comparable to some other mountain elevations on the island. I gazed out from the summits of the two Bubbles only briefly, and I managed to make my way over to Bubble Rock, a large glacial erratic, a boulder that differs from the surrounding rocks and is believed to have been brought from a distance by glacial action. Bubble Rock sits precariously on the eastern side of South Bubble's summit and attracts a good deal of attention from sightseers below on the road. After allowing myself only a few minutes of gazing at my next peak to climb, I was on my way down the trail. Five mountains were in the bag; only one remained.

Pemetic Mountain, at 1,248 feet in elevation, rises above the eastern shore of Jordan Pond and gets its name from the early Native American name for the Mount Desert Island area, "Pemetic," which means "sloping land." It's the third highest summit in Acadia National Park, and the views of Bubble Rock, Jordan Pond, Cadillac Mountain, Seal Harbor, Somes Sound, and the Cranberry Islands from the summit are expansive and inspiring. This was my final summit destination. Perhaps it was because it was my sixth mountain, and I was getting tired, but I found this trail to be the most demanding. Roots protruded around loose rock and the trees seemed closer on the trail. It took longer than I estimated to reach the summit, but I eventually made it. Mid-afternoon had come and gone, the balls of my feet were starting to ache, I was hot, and I was thinking about how good it would feel to get back to my motel room and jump in the pool. I was very satisfied with my accomplishments that day, but I was also very ready to be off the trails.

I could feel the hike down in my quads and on the balls of my feet. The trail descended through the evergreens, joined up with a wide, carriage/equestrian road made of stone dust, and finally deposited me at the Jordan Pond House parking lot where I had parked my car several hours earlier. I began to think how good a fresh lemonade from the restaurant would taste, so as I arrived at my car, I unzipped my pack to get my wallet.

"Hmmm…that's odd," I thought. My wallet wasn't in my pack. But it had to be. I clearly remembered dropping it into my pack at the Precipice parking lot before I climbed Champlain. I checked again, emptying my entire pack's contents onto the rear seat of my rental car. No wallet. I checked the car…under the seats, between the seats and the doors, even in places I hadn't opened like the glove compartment. Still…nothing. Frustrated and with panic beginning to set in, I checked everywhere several more times, and I began to think where it might have disappeared. I hadn't even opened my pack during the hikes. My water bottles were on the outer pockets of my pack. Then I remembered. I had opened my pack — just once — on the summit of Champlain Mountain to get a piece of gum. My wallet must have fallen out in the morning on the mountain's summit. It was the only explanation I could imagine, but I also knew what that meant; I had to climb Champlain again. This time I had to climb the north trail because it was faster and easier.

I jumped in the car, made my way out of the parking lot, and headed for the eastern shore of Mount Desert Island and the Champlain trailhead. While I was driving, the panic intensified because the reality of my situation began to sink into my consciousness. I was in Maine with no money, no credit cards, no identification, and no driver's license. I literally had nothing except the clothes and pack on my back. If I didn't find my wallet, how was I going to eat? How was I going to pay for my room? How was I going to get home? I flew to Maine, which meant I needed identification to fly home. I couldn't prove who I was in a place where nobody knew me. Then I started to think about my wallet. What if someone else found it? Would it be turned in to the police? Would my credit cards and money still be there? Could it have fallen into a crevice where no one could see it or find it, including me? Admittedly, I wasn't very calm about the situation, so I was thankful when I arrived at the parking area and found a spot to park.

Springing out of the car, I grabbed a water bottle and the keys, and took off down the road to the trailhead. Although it was late in the afternoon and I was tired and this was my second time up Champlain that day, I found myself running up the northern flanks of the mountain. I was praying the whole way up. "God, please let me find this wallet. I don't know what I'll do if I can't find it. Please…I'm in a real jam here!" I passed several families on their way down the trail, and I could only imagine the number of people who had scoured the summit since my morning climb. Up I went, sweating and filled with worry and crying out to God in my mind for help.

It's a very vulnerable feeling being stripped of identity and currency when one is away from home. Without even change for a phone call, I knew I was in trouble. Everything rested on me finding my wallet on this climb. Everything came down to this one site. It was either there, or it wasn't.

I rounded a bend in the trail, now well out of the tree line and I could see the summit. My goal was in sight, perhaps only three hundred yards away, when I passed a man sitting on a boulder to the right of the trail. I noticed he was dressed in rather drab clothing that fit the profile of a late-nineteenth-century hiker, the kind one sees on those prints by the Hudson Valley painters. This man appeared to be about sixty years old with a rather long, grey beard, and he was wearing a long-sleeved linen shirt with an earthen-toned bandana of sorts underneath his collar, brown wool vest and matching long pants, and a generic pair of high-laced, leather hiking boots. He sported a brimmed hat, which was on his knee, a knapsack, and he held a wooden hiking staff in his hand. "What an unusual looking character," I thought as I approached him, and it occurred to me that I should ask if he was on his way up or down the mountain. If he had already been at the summit, he might have seen or maybe even found my wallet at the top. However, I decided against it, thinking it would use up time, and spare time was something I didn't have. As I ran by this man, he called out to me.

"Fine afternoon for a hike," he said. This made me stop and turn toward him.

"It is," I responded. "Have you been to the top?"

"Sure have. Beautiful, isn't it? God knew what he was doing when he made Acadia."

"I agree. You didn't happen to see a wallet on the top did you? I lost mine this morning."

"No, I didn't…"

"Okay," I said, cutting him off. "Thank you." And I turned to continue to the summit.

"But you know," he continued, "you might want to check in at the park entrance by Schooner Head. The rangers there will be helpful."

I waved in gratitude for his suggestion, and continued to the summit.

When I arrived at the top, there were three people sitting in the late afternoon sun and appreciating the views. I went straight for the place where I opened my pack. There was no trace of my wallet at all. I searched a ten foot radius around the place where I rested earlier in the day and even asked the people at the top if anyone had found it. No one had seen my wallet. It was gone, and by then I was out of my mind with concern. Then I remembered the old hiker's suggestion. The park entrance huts…maybe…just maybe. It was worth checking. Three minutes or so after arriving at the summit, I began to race down the same trail I had just ascended.

Scrambling over open rock, I passed the location where the hiker had offered his advice, but he was gone. He had probably continued his climb down the mountain, but I remember finding it odd that I didn't see him ahead of me considering the exposed nature of the mountain. "I'll pass him on the way down for sure," I thought. After all, I was traveling light and running most of the way. Although my wallet was certainly occupying most of my thoughts, I kept finding it odd that I wasn't seeing any trace of the old hiker. The lower I got, the more odd it seemed. Eventually I got to the road and the car.

31

The old hiker had vanished. There was literally no way anyone could have come down the mountain faster than me and no way I wouldn't have passed him. There is a trail that leads to the east, but even that trail junction was far beyond the point where I should have passed this man. It was as if he had literally disappeared, and, despite my wallet concerns, I found it a bit unnerving.

Getting into the car, I drove ahead to the entrance of the park loop, pulled the car into an empty space, and walked up to one of the two huts. Inside was a single ranger whose task it was to check and sell park passes while welcoming people in the entering vehicles. I knocked on his door, expecting this to be a brief encounter leading to another dead end. When he answered, I gave my name to the ranger and explained my situation to him. He admitted that nobody had turned in a wallet to the entrance station, but he offered to call over to the park headquarters located at the center of the island.

As he got on the phone, I stood outside, listening to his end of the conversation through the hut's open window.

"I'd like to check to see if anyone turned in a wallet today," the ranger inquired.

I was ready for the "no" to come very quickly, but it didn't. It got interesting.

"Gordon T. Ward. New Jersey. Really?"

You've got to be kidding me, I thought. It can't be.

"Mmm-hmm. About lunchtime? Really?"

My heart was about to leap out of my chest with anticipation at this point. It sounded very promising.

"Okay, I'll let him know." The ranger hung up and opened the door to the hut. "You're in luck," he said with a smile. "Another ranger turned in your wallet just after lunch. It's waiting for you at the park headquarters.

Relief is not even a word that comes close to describing what I felt. Suddenly, I had identification. I had money and credit.

I could fly back to New Jersey. My worries were gone, and I couldn't wait to ask who returned it and where it was found.

When I got to park headquarters, I went to the front desk and explained who I was. Sure enough, I was handed my wallet, intact with all of my ID, credit cards, and cash. Thanking the woman behind the desk profusely, I asked, "Do you know who returned this and where it was found?"

"Ranger McDaniel, one of the rangers assigned to the Precipice trailhead found it this morning. She brought it here around noon."

"Can you tell me where I can find her? I'd like to thank her."

"She's off duty now," she said. Chances are she's at the apartments in the old gatehouse over by the Jordan Pond stables. I can give you directions if you'd like."

"No need," I said, "I know exactly where the gatehouse is. Thank you so much!"

I turned and walked out, wallet in hand, feeling so good, and knowing where I was going next...back to Jordan Pond. By that time, it was getting near to 6:00 p.m., so when I arrived at the gatehouse, I wasn't sure if anyone would be there. I knocked on the door. When a woman answered, I asked if Ranger McDaniel was there and explained why I wanted to see her. In a few minutes, a young woman came to the door and introduced herself as Michelle. Her story restored my faith in humanity.

As it turns out, Michelle was one of the rangers I had met that morning while she was running the Peregrine falcon watch. She had noticed a wallet on the parking lot after I drove away to climb my other five mountains that morning. Picking it up, she not only recognized my face on the driver's license, she remembered the color and type of car I was driving. What's more, when she was finished with her activity, Michelle drove around most of the park trying to find my car with the hope of returning the wallet to me! I was amazed that anyone would do this. When she didn't find me or my car, she resorted to dropping it off at the ranger headquarters.

Now, I may never know just why Michelle remembered my car and face out of all the people she saw that morning, but the more the events of that day rolled around in my head, the more astounded I became. It was the old-fashioned hiker that stuck in my mind. I knew about the Acadia National Park Information Center, but I didn't know that a rangers' headquarters even existed. Honestly, I can't say that I would have checked there if that bearded hiker hadn't spoken to me and suggested that I inquire at the park entrance. Then there's the strange apparel he was wearing and the way he seemed to vanish without a trace on the rock face of that exposed trail. And why did he mention how God knew what he was doing when he made Acadia?

The more I thought about it, the more I had the feeling that this hiker wasn't flesh and blood. I believe he was an angel, one that was sent as a direct answer to my prayers. God worked through Michelle that day by inspiring her to search for me and then to bring the wallet to headquarters, but God also knew I needed direction. I needed to be shown where to look, so He sent an angel to Champlain that afternoon, an angel to be my compass on that day of trails and mountains.

Memories in the Mist

The early, fog-shrouded morning along the beach of Marlboro, Maine, has a personality and a beauty all its own. Hidden in the murkiness are the calls of loons and gulls and the intermittent whir of a lobsterman's winch and the groaning song of his boat's engine. They cannot be seen, but I know exactly where they are. Raccoon Cove calls to them the way it calls to me, beckoning us to explore and know it more intimately, and so it was that I shook the dream-laden cobwebs from my mind, wiped the sleep from my eyes, and slipped on my shoes for a run to the beach. I hadn't even reached the top of the driveway before the fog had enveloped me and eclipsed the cottage at my back.

The route I took is one I know by heart, having traced and retraced it countless times since I was eight years old. Alone in the fog, my footsteps kept me company as ghostly apparitions of alder and red spruce trees continually appeared alongside the shoulder of the road and receded into the fog. Rounding the bend in the road that leads to the beach, the surface changes from macadam to gravel over hard-packed dirt and then to sand, and the sound of my footfalls shifted accordingly from slaps, to crunches, and finally to that soft shoosh of feet running in powder. The beach itself was edged by wild roses. Within the grey blanket around me, the white foam and sound of the lapping waves were the only markers that delineated where the beach ended and the water began.

Deep in thought, memories flooded my mind, and I realized I no longer ran alone. So much had happened to me on this beach over the years, and the people with whom I shared the events materialised from memory to accompany me one at a time. There's a point where the beach turns from sand to rounded rocks, perfect for a little boy to go rock hopping. It's here where my pace slowed, and my grandmother, alive again, came out of the mist to warn me, as she had done so often, "Don't run on the rocks, Gordie. You'll break your ankle." I smiled and listened, but I still hopped on the rocks. I glimpsed my daughter with a delighted smile on her face after successfully skipping a flat stone across the surface of the rippled water. Out on the cove, I recalled how my son turned to me from the front cockpit of our kayak, eager to show me the enormous sea star he had just lifted out of the water. Glancing toward the head of the beach, my wife, looking as peaceful as I've ever seen her, held out her hand and smiled at me from the base of Whale Rock.

Continuing to leaf through the pages of time, I saw my first girlfriend walking along the water's edge, holding my hand as we navigated the slippery rocks. No sooner had she faded into the mist than my father appeared, helping me as a child into our rowboat and easing us into the water of the cove to go fishing. Before long, I realized I was almost home, and there in my mind's eye was my daughter again, only this time she was thirteen months old. We sat on a white boulder, her in my lap, and I baptized her with the water from the cove. Turning away from this scene, I saw the beach stairs to home ascending into the fog, but as I looked up, my mother appeared, smiling down at me from the top, an apron full of rose hips she had picked to make jelly. As I climbed toward her, the bittersweet image of my mother receded into the grey fog and was replaced by that of our cottage overlooking the water. My companions drifted back into time and the murky mist of the beach. I could no longer see them, but I knew they would always reside there.

Three weeks earlier, before I left for my annual trip to Maine, I was chatting about my upcoming visit with a saleswoman at a farm market near my home. She said she didn't understand why anyone would want to go back to the same location more than once when there are so many other places to see. I considered her position and then responded, "Why are you married?" Then she understood. When one deeply loves a person or a place, there are endless delights and rewards found in discovering and creating limitless layers of shared experience. There's also a peace and a comfort found in the familiarity of that which speaks to one's soul.

As life changes, memories keep us connected to everyone and everything we've found in this life and, perhaps, even further back, to the breath of creation. That morning in Maine after my run, while I stood in the heavy fog and stretched at the head of the beach stairs, I wondered to myself. If I could remember back far enough, would my earliest memory be that of God? Could we recall the moments when the hand of creation swept us into this world. I feel as if I could, because I know that creative force is still at work within me. It's within all of us. We may not see it with our eyes, but it's something very real we can feel beside and within us. We do not run alone through life. Like my memories from the beach, our Creator never leaves our sides, shrouded in the mist of certainty between Earth and the vast sea of eternity.

The Nine Faces of God

The divine is constantly at work in our lives. Sometimes this divinity can be so close that the presence becomes tangible. Can we recognize the miraculous amid the mundane? At what point do we stop and consider that we are in the company of angels and that events are not mere chance?

During the summer of 1994, a good friend of mine Todd Paige and I cycled, hiked, and canoed 1,800 miles of the historic Lewis and Clark Trail from Bismarck, North Dakota, to Seaside, Oregon. Our expedition was dubbed *Quest West*. We originally did this to raise money for a school scholarship, but, once on the trail, we realized very quickly that it was to become one of the most significant adventures of our lives. In fact, it was a watershed experience for my faith development.

Miracles and *Godincidences* were things I figured happened to other people. The belief that God would be fully present in my life never seemed likely to me, but I was about to find out differently. It all began as we approached the open rangeland of central Montana, and it continued though our descent out of the Bitterroot Mountains in Idaho. Time after time, events transpired that left no doubt in my mind that we were not alone on our trip. Looking back on it, there was an unseen presence, angels, God, call it what you will, caring for us on our expedition, and the ways in which this presence made itself known to us were truly amazing.

What follows are some of my original, daily, journal entry accounts of our miraculous adventures, most of which were documented at the end of each day's events. However, when one is immersed in an experience, it is sometimes difficult to see the big picture. For that reason, these entries have been augmented to include the larger perspectives that can only be gained from looking back on the entire expedition, although the seeds of these perspectives were definitely sprouting and taking root in my mind at the time these events occurred.

The Storm
June 26, 1994, Sunday

What a magnificent Sunday this was! We packed at our support vehicle—which we called the *Rig*—at Fort Peck, MT, and listened to the weather forecast on the radio, which called for a big thunderstorm with dangerous hail. The last storm of such magnitude was accompanied by grapefruit-sized hail that damaged roofs and cars, not to mention what it could do to people. We had nothing to protect us except our bike helmets, and they wouldn't offer our bodies much protection from five-inch diameter chunks of ice falling from the sky.

Eventually, the storm reports subsided, and, seeing no trace of clouds in the sky, both Todd and I were eager to get on our bikes. The decision was made to head out into open rangeland around 2:30 in the afternoon. We said goodbye to Bob, our support vehicle driver, and agreed that we would meet him several days later at the James Kipp Recreation Area.

Our ride began at the intersection of Seventh Ridge Road and Willow Creek Road with an expansive, 360-degree horizon and no trace of any other people. It was sunny when we began, but a ridge of clouds in the west signaled an approaching change in the weather. Thirty minutes into our ride, we began to see dust blowing on the road far ahead of us, and it was coming toward us. We figured it was a car or truck traveling at a good rate of speed and kicking up dirt in its path. As it got nearer, Todd and I realized that there was no vehicle approaching us; it was wind.

Several minutes after this realization, it hit. The dust storm blew hard up the once seemingly endless dirt road, shortening its linear character with grey and brown haze. Todd and I pulled into a grass covered "road," indicated only by tire marks that flattened the existing grass, and we unpacked our shelter. Wind hammered away at the formless tent, turning it into a sail, which we desperately fought to erect. Grey-black clouds suffocated the once blue skies above us and to the west. One is quickly reminded how small we are compared to the awesome power of nature on this open grazing rangeland.

Eventually, the tent was up, and we hurriedly threw our panniers inside to weigh it down. Sandblasted bikes were dragged behind the tent to shield them from the wind-driven dirt, and we crawled inside the stretched fabric form that was being battered and pushed to one side by the storm — still no rain, just the constant driving wind. I was a bit nervous. After all, we were the tallest feature around us, totally exposed on this open rangeland and facing a fierce electrical storm and surrounded by aluminum poles.

We hoped for the best and hunkered down to face the tempest, but as we looked out the tent door we noticed an incredible occurrence, an event that I would consider to be our first miracle. The storm started to move in a clockwise pattern, swirling directly above our tent and leaving clear skies above us. We were being miraculously spared and only received a few sprinkles as we watched violent lightning strikes and sheets of rain fall to the south, north, and east upon the open rangeland. Continuing for perhaps thirty minutes or so, the relentless rain barraged the land around us, but left us relatively unscathed.

Although the wind never stopped, we managed to cook an evening meal, and, afterwards, we had an entertaining time chasing the free-roaming, open-range cattle away from our tent. They were extremely curious and much bigger than us! In addition, another spectacular gift was given to us in the form of an unexpected sunset which contrasted the brightly lit, golden buttes to the east against the dark, grey skies. The spectacle was stunning and breathtaking! This is a moment that you have to experience to truly appreciate, and we were fortunate to have been given a chance to view it. We thought we were going to get hammered by a storm, and we didn't. I don't know why the storm missed us, but I began to get the feeling that an unseen presence was guarding and protecting us.

After a long and varied day, we went to bed at 9:45 p.m. because we planned to get up early and make it to Sun Prairie. I feared we hadn't escaped the storm in its entirety, as the skies began to look more menacing again after sunset. It is hard to describe the total isolation and vulnerability that one feels out there, especially in the face of threatening weather, but I caught myself pondering, more than once, the possibility of being protected by a guiding, unseen force. As time wore on, I found these thoughts crept into my consciousness more and more.

The Road Grader
June 27, 1994, Monday

I woke up thinking about my daughter Melina, for it was her seventh birthday, and I wished terribly that I could have been with her back in New Jersey. Happy birthday, Mina! I did not sleep well during the night and thought constantly about the possibility of getting to a phone, so I could call her on her birthday.

The rain showers were intermittent during the night, but the rain, which had died off in the early evening of the 26th, resumed its fury around 2:30 a.m. The rain on the tent was a very lonely sound, and Todd and I both felt extremely isolated. A vehicle of some sort drove past us at 4:30 a.m. We were in our tent and did not see it, but we wondered where the person might be headed in such a lonesome and far removed area.

I got up at 4:59 a.m., as did Todd, and we cooked a breakfast of oatmeal. The sky was grey, and the wind was driving and consistent. After we ate, we donned our rain gear, packed, and started dismantling our tent. Suddenly the sound of an engine was heard, and a yellow pickup truck came over the rise and pulled into our site. A weathered-looking man that exuded a confidence of the surrounding area rolled down his window and asked in a gravelly voice, "What are you doing way the hell out here?" I explained that we were caught in the storm, and we described the ordeal we had setting up the tent. We also asked about the road we planned to follow that led to Sun Prairie, and the man's response was, "Nooo, I don't think they use that road anymore."

"What do you mean? We have USGS maps that show a road. Are you sure?" I asked.

"Trust me son," he said, "there's no road there...used to be, but not anymore."

Well, needless to say, this piece of information was to make all the difference in our trip, since we would have surely run into problems with our intended route. He gave us directions for a more traveled road, whatever "traveled" meant, and we noted his directions. Before he drove off, we asked him where he was going. "To work!" was his reply, and he drove off into the early morning light. Where he could possibly work in the middle of open rangeland was a mystery to us, but we were to be given an answer very soon. Our chance meeting would come to be viewed by myself as one which seemed to have been arranged by fate, or maybe even God. If I was not convinced about the existence of angels at this point, I would soon be faced with a series of events that would make me reconsider.

Todd and I finished dismantling our weather beaten tent, packed our belongings and proceeded west on the muddy Willow Creek Road. Our first mile was rough because of the relentless headwind. When we came to the intersection with the road to Sun Prairie, and I use the terms "intersection" and "road" very loosely, we spotted the yellow truck that our early morning visitor had been driving, but there was no sign of him anywhere. Jokingly, Todd and I mentioned that he must have been abducted by aliens because there was literally nothing around us for as far as we could see, only open rangeland. Where could this man have possibly gone?

At any rate, we took the advice that our "guide" had given us earlier in the day and turned right, heading up the alternate, serpentine, dirt road named Stone House Road. Todd and I were prepared for the fact that we would not see any paved roads for a couple of days, but this dirt was thick from the rain, and it stuck to our tires like glue. The local folks call this mud "gumbo."

About 300 yards up this road, we encountered our first piece of "bad luck" for the day. My rear tire had gone flat, and we were forced to stop while I unpacked my gear and removed the rear wheel and tire. Of course, the wind was still blowing hard, the skies were still overcast, and we were hoping that it would not rain during this episode. The dirt, which I had mentioned earlier, now stuck to everything it touched, and the most maddening part was trying to keep our cleats from becoming encased in it. Of course, our efforts were in vain. I tried three times to patch the inner tube but had no luck in getting the patch to stick. It was also very difficult to determine where the leaks were, as the sound of escaping air from the inner tube was easily drowned out by the wind.

During the last try, Todd spotted a vehicle in the distance that seemed to be coming our way, albeit very slowly. We continued working but kept an eye on whatever was approaching because it didn't seem to be a car. Finally it got close enough for us to determine that it was a road grader. Apparently, someone had the job of scraping all of the foot-high weeds off of the crest of the road. When it got to us, it stopped, and we saw that the driver was none other than our morning visitor. He shook his head, took the cigarette from his lips, and asked us if we needed help. With blind pride, Todd and I both thanked him but said that we would be fine. Actually, we had already decided to scrap the original inner tube and replace it with a new one. Our friend nodded in acceptance and continued his seemingly endless grading, leaving us with no idea about how important this meeting was going to prove to be.

Our new tubes ended up being a little too small for our rims, but this particular one worked, at least for the time being. Todd and I sipped some water, which was getting low after a day of no water sources, reassembled my bike and resumed our riding, thinking how odd it was to have met the same man in less than a few hours in this unpopulated environment. Both times he showed up when he was or might have been needed most.

Our new route presented two problems. One was the additional miles, which we would have to pedal in order to make it to the James Kipp Recreation Area by tomorrow afternoon. That alone was a considerable obstacle considering the vicious headwinds that were seriously hampering our progress. The second issue was that neither Bob nor anyone else would know our new route should we run into trouble. We had been forced to cut our support line in order to make it to our next designated meeting point, and there were no towns at all through which we would be passing, only a small dot on the map called Stone House. This all meant that we had to push ourselves hard to make up the miles, and we had to be very careful in the process.

All day we rode into the same headwind, and, although the skies cleared, we were growing more and more concerned about our situation. We were surrounded in every direction and as far as we could see by rolling terrain that was covered by grey rock, brown dirt, and yellow clover. Nowhere was there any sign of water. The wind often changed direction but not intensity, so our tire tracks looked like the tracks of snakes, crisscrossing the road as if we were drunken men. Just as we gained stability with one direction of the wind, it would shift and slam into us from another direction. The combination of the hills, an increasing lack of water, an even more increasing desire to drink, and the variable wind sapped our strength quickly. Our two-way radio would not reach Bob, and there were no cells in the area to carry the signal for the cellular phone. Except for our "friend" working in the road grader, we had not seen another person, or the sign of another person, all day. As we were told, "No one goes out there." All we could do was plod onward and look forward to the chance that the place marked Stone House on our map would have a phone.

Six hours after we had started our ride, we had covered only 10.67 miles, averaging 1.94 miles per hour in vicious headwinds. At one point Todd got off of his bike as we were climbing a hill and kept pace with me by walking as I rode. There was nothing that could have prepared us for this, and the emotional drain was tremendous because of the uncertainty of our route and the urgency of our situation.

As we came over the top of one of the many hills, we saw what we had been hoping to see…water! It wasn't much. In fact, it was only a drainage pool about 30 yards in diameter, but it was water nonetheless. We worked our way down the hill into

45

the wind and wasted no time getting the water purifier pump out of the pannier. Trudging through the ankle deep mud that surrounded the drainage pool, we noticed a pair of American Avocet birds, which we had disturbed. They flew around the pool of water constantly, nervously landing for only a few seconds before taking to flight again. They were interesting birds to see, as they resembled large sandpipers with long, curved beaks and blue legs. They most likely had a nest in the area.

Anyway, Todd volunteered to walk into the mud and water far enough to get to a depth where the purifier would work. This was a new purifier, which had been used only once by Todd after he ordered it. Imagine our total disbelief when it would not work correctly! Water spurted out of the top of the unit instead of running through the tube. Emotions ran the gamut from frustration to infuriation and from contemplation to fright as we considered our situation—windy, 90° heat, no form of communication for help, nobody knew where we were, and no water. To drink the unpurified water would mean running the risk of contracting Giardia, an intestinal parasite, which would certainly end the journey for both of us. To not drink any water would mean serious trouble, and we tried not to think about it. We certainly didn't talk about it, but we could see the worry in each other's eyes.

Getting back to my earlier comment on angels... A series of events, which had played themselves out unbeknownst to us, was about to affect us in a wondrous manner. As Todd and I were feeling about as frightened and discouraged as we had ever been, I looked up the road to see a spectacular sight. Coming over the rise of the road was an RV, our Rig, which paused at the top of the hill, so that Bob could get out and take a photograph of us. Even he did not yet know the gravity of our situation and how well timed his unexpected appearance was.

As soon as Bob pulled the Rig up to us and we quenched our thirsts, we wasted no time in asking Bob how he found us.

Apparently the storm from the previous night had missed us but had hammered other locations with torrential rains, violent lightning, hail the size of quarters, and heavy winds. Bob became extremely worried for our safety and set out looking for us at daybreak. He followed our designated route, only to find, as we had been told, that the road leading to Sun Prairie was closed. Retracing his route, Bob remarkably happened to pass another vehicle, a road grader operated by no other than our morning visitor who was still at work grading the dirt roads. Not only did Bob stop to speak with him, but because of our meeting earlier in the morning, our friend recognized us by Bob's descriptions, told him where we were headed, described our route, and said that we had had problems with our tires. Had it not been for that guide in the pickup truck on his way to work, we would have been in a very grave situation. He was the only person that would have known our whereabouts. Were all of these events coincidences? We felt very fortunate, and I again sensed the comforting impression that someone was watching over us.

Continuing our journey in the Rig, we headed toward a town named Saco. It was amazing to see how differently Todd and I now viewed the environment. From the relative safety and security of the RV, the land suddenly took on a beautiful, scenic quality that had not impressed us before. Along the way, we saw a rattlesnake on the dusty road, a reminder of the other risks involved with our trip. Oh, and we did pass that place called Stone House, and it is a good thing that we didn't depend upon this location for a telephone and water, for it was not a town. It was, as the name suggested, nothing more than an abandoned stone house. We saw some free-roaming horses in the vicinity but no people at all.

Finally we got to Saco and had to fill up on gas, which had become another concern of ours for a time. We saw no place for lunch, so we continued driving to a town called Malta. Our rule for eating was one that we adopted from our friend Dayton Duncan, who had driven the Lewis and Clark Trail.

The best places to eat are those that have someone's name on the sign. No chain or franchise restaurants are allowed, but diners are acceptable.

There was a diner in Malta that had a casino attached to it. Understand that this was not your Las Vegas/Atlantic City type of casino. These establishments reminded me more of bowling alleys, and slot machines were the main attraction. Todd and I had burgers, fries, and shakes, and what a welcome sight they were! After eating, I called one of our equipment suppliers in Bedminster, New Jersey, and asked them to send inner tubes that might better fit our off-road tires. They agreed to send them to the outfitter where we would soon arrive for our Missouri River canoe trip.

Again, it was time to drive, and we headed down to the James Kipp Recreation Area. It took a while, but we arrived in the mid-afternoon. This gave us time to look around the scenic campsite and take in some time beside the river. Magpies were very abundant here and were stunning with their black and white coloring.

Todd and I plan to bike east along the river tomorrow in order to take in some of the sights that we would have seen on our original route. This meant cleaning our bikes before dinner, since they were covered with red dust from our ride out of the Fort Peck rangeland. After dealing with a drainage problem in the RV's shower and organizing our gear for tomorrow's overnight trip, I am certain that we are all looking forward to a solid night's sleep!

The Water-Bearers of Lolo
July 15, 1994, Friday (written on the morning of July 16, 1994)

Yesterday was our first day on the Lolo Trail, the old, Native American trail that Lewis and Clark used to traverse the Bitterroot section of Rocky Mountains, guided by a group from the Shoshone tribe. Our morning started with a huge breakfast in, of all places, the Missoula airport. We had had a great breakfast there on Tuesday and figured that it was very near the RV repair center where we needed to bring our Rig. Bob had flown back to New Jersey, and Todd's wife Susie had flown in to join us for this backpacking portion of the trip.

In order to allow our next support driver to fly in and meet us at the end of the trail five days later, Todd, Susie, and I were able to secure a ride into the Bitterroot Mountains to the beginning of the Wendover Ridge Trail. It is located just three miles west of the Powell Ranger Station on Route 12 in Idaho where each of us filled up our two water bottles. While we were there, we did stop to ask the ranger on duty about the trail, noting that we were using the Wendover Trail to access the Lolo Trail, which we expected to travel on for five days.

"Well," he explained to us, "the top of the trail was difficult to follow, but if we kept heading north along the ridge, we would be fine. Oh, and by the way, nobody ever really does that, you know."

"Does what?" we asked.

"Hike the Lolo Trail."

Extremely surprised at this statement, we asked why this was the case. It was, after all, a historic trail.

"Lots of folks use it," he responded, "but few do the entire trail, and the ones that do go by horse or four-wheel-drive truck. There's not much water up there, and they need the vehicles and horses to carry the water. Nobody really hikes up there."

Then the ranger said something that would soon prove to be very meaningful. "You probably won't see more than three or four trucks the whole time you're up there."

Undaunted, we explained that we had done our homework and identified streams and other water sources where we could find water for our journey, and we confidently walked across Route 12 and started up the Wendover Ridge Trail.

As the ranger had warned us, the trail was poorly marked, but the path was well worn and easily followed. However, the trail was very steep with a 3,200-foot increase in elevation and a relentless climb shrouded in dense Red spruce and Lodgepole pine. We found ourselves thankful that we had our water, always keeping an eye out for the streams and rivulets that were indicated on the map for pumping more when needed.

We soon reached a logging road and followed the trail across the road, pausing only while Todd treated blisters on the backs of his heels. Still the trail climbed, and we eventually approached the intersection with an even older logging road, now overgrown, where we were told it was easy to lose the trail. We did. The first path that we took led to a dead end, at a cliff, and the second, although affording us spectacular views, began to lead off the ridge. Remembering that the trail followed the ridge line, I eventually found the Wendover Ridge Trail by dropping my pack and bushwhacking up toward the crest of the ridge. After we all got back on the trail, we decided to rest at a clear, level spot for lunch. We were all tired and looking forward to passing the Lewis and Clark Wendover Ridge Rest Site, as this marked the halfway point on the trail.

After about thirty minutes, we continued our hike. It was very hot, and we were running short on water and miserable from the steep climb. What we didn't know at the time was that the summer of 1994 would prove to be a time of drought in the Bitterroot Mountains. Not knowing this, we surmised that the streams indicated on our map were seasonal, as we found no rivulets or streams at all. On September 15, 1805, William Clark noted a similar difficulty in finding water after his climb up Wendover Ridge and had to melt the snow they found at the top. There was one point where I considered going back, since we were half way through our water supply, the heat continued to build, and there wasn't a hint of another water source anywhere. Todd's legs were shaking, and Susie and I were feeling weak. We knew that if we continued to head north, eventually we would have to cross the Lolo Trail, also known as dirt road number 500. The trail seemed to stretch on and up forever, we hadn't passed the Rest Site, which was supposed to be marked, and we were feeling frustrated, weak, and worried about our health and supply of water. We were already dehydrated. Little did we know that our lunch site was actually the Lewis and Clark Wendover Ridge Rest Site. It would seem that the same moderation in grade, which persuaded the famous explorers to choose this as a resting site, had the same influence on the three of us.

The uphill battle continued, and all three of us were severely dehydrated and utterly exhausted. Suddenly Susie spotted a small, wooden sign, and I saw the rough, dirt road, the Lolo Trail! We rejoiced at the knowledge that we had reached our goal and were finally off the Wendover Ridge Trail. Actually we were quite giddy, and I felt good about being able to pinpoint our location on the map. We dropped our frame packs and collapsed on the side of the Lolo Trail, relishing in a moment of rest. Still, we knew that we had to find water—and quickly! During our hike, we had made a plan. Todd was to hike east for fifteen minutes, scouting for water. I was to hike west doing the same thing, and Susie was going to stay on the trail with our frame packs. In a half hour, we would meet and choose the best direction to go to secure water.

Then something amazing happened. Todd and I had already run into a situation where we encountered an "angel" above

Fort Peck Lake in the form of a road grader driver. Now it was something else. Understand that only three vehicles or so, on the average, were said to travel along the Lolo Trail during our trip. Unbelievably, just as we had dropped our packs and sat to ponder our plan, we heard an engine.

Looking toward our right, a car appeared over the crest of the hill to the east. This was not a truck—this was a blue, late model sedan. The car slowed, then stopped in front of us. All three of us rose to our feet and approached the car. There was a man in the passenger seat, and a woman was driving. We greeted them and were about to ask if they had passed or noticed any water source when the man said, "You know, there's not much water up here." While disturbing, this news saved us a trip, since we had planned to split up in order to find a source of water.

The really miraculous part happened next. The woman said, "You look thirsty." As she was saying this, she proceeded to reach down between her car seats and then gave us an entire seltzer bottle, which had been refilled with fresh, cool water. As if that weren't enough, the couple then told us that there was a good spring, a water source, three miles up the trail to the west. Needless to say, we were dumfounded, and after thanking them, they simply drove slowly out of sight.

Todd and Susie and I just stood there looking at each other and the water bottle. "What are the chances of that occurring?" we asked ourselves. "Were these two individuals people or angels? Was this meeting chance, circumstance, or fate?" Whichever was the case, we definitely felt a chill run up our spines. I started to think about the timing of these two people and what it takes to get people ready to pack up for a day on the trail. Just imagine the complexity of possibilities...

Honey, where's that shirt you washed?

Do you want coffee?

Let's stop for gas.

Whoops! That was a wrong turn.

There are a myriad of items that affected these people's timing. If they had been a minute earlier, we would have missed each other. If we had stopped just once more to rest on our ascent or lingered a minute longer on one of our breaks, we would have missed them. What we witnessed was a miracle. I believe these two individuals were angels. We were being cared for by an unseen partner on this journey, and in that meeting, the invisible was made visible for us. I think we were all pretty much in agreement on that.

After partially satisfying our thirst by sharing the water we had been given, we put our backpacks on and headed west down the Lolo Trail, which, at this point, was a dirt road. Sure enough, we passed a stream in about three miles — clear and cold water and plenty of it, just as we had been told by the couple in the car. We filled our water bottles, pushed liquids by drinking a quart each, and refilled our bottles again.

By now it was 6:00 p.m., and we needed to find a campsite. All of the land was sloped, so it was hard to find a suitable location. Our feet hurt, and we were hoping to find one soon. I imagine we walked about 1.5 miles further, and I finally spotted a place up off the right side of the road. That was it. We set up camp and ate noodles and chicken with mixed vegetables out on a rocky point overlooking the surrounding mountains and forest. What a spectacular sight!

After hanging our food, we all crawled into the tent for a well-deserved night's sleep. During the night, we were awakened by three distinct events. The first was the sound of a deer or elk running down the dirt road beneath us. The second was the sound of a man, somewhere in the distance around midnight, screaming "hey!" a dozen or so times. This was followed, about twenty minutes later, by a truck that drove down the motorway. I was glad to be up above the road where our tent could not be seen, especially after learning a week later that the Lolo Trail is part of a network of trails and logging roads that are used by drug runners who travel by night attempting to move drugs up into Canada. If we had made contact with the likes of them by camping lower on the slope, one can only guess what may have happened. We could have simply disappeared in the mountains. The last interruption was the sound of a deer's warning signal, sounding much like a loud cough, below us in the forest. I finally dozed off to sleep thinking that we were going to be okay. How could we not? God was with us.

Vision on the Hill

July 16, 1994, Saturday

I slept on and off last night, and finally decided to get up at 5:30 a.m. on Saturday, July 16. It was going to be another sunny day. After filling in a few details on yesterday's journal entry this morning, Todd and Susie were also awake, and we had a breakfast of freeze-dried blueberry pancakes, sausage, and instant oatmeal. It wasn't what you would expect from a restaurant, but it served its purpose. We then packed up and went back up the trail to the spring that we had passed the day before. Since we don't know what lies ahead in terms of water, it was decided that we had better fill up before leaving.

The hiking was very slow today. We left at 9:45 a.m. in bright sunshine. Our feet hurt and Todd's blisters were bad. Our hips were also uncomfortable from the hip belts of our frame packs. We covered about seven miles today, half of which were uphill. We passed no water, so we were thankful that we had filled our bottles in the morning. While backpacking, our attention was totally focused on listening for the sound of running water. Sometimes we would be fooled by the sound of the wind in the tops of the trees, but mostly it was silent…a silence broken only by our rhythmic footsteps and the occasional cry of a raven, chickadee, or jay.

Eventually, we came to a spot that Lewis and Clark had named Bear Oil and Roots, its namesake being the ingredients of a meal that the explorers had here while they camped on June 27, 1806. As we came to expect, there was no sign, but there were two signposts where a sign was intended to be installed. We have found these trails and sites to be extremely poorly marked, but I understand that there is an effort to install signage on the entire trail in time for the 200th anniversary of the Lewis and Clark expedition. The good part about this site was that there was a spring that ran out of a drainage pipe at the edge of the road. All of us drank a full bottle of water and refilled all of our bottles.

As it was now 2:00 p.m., it was decided that we should stay at this location for the night. This place gave us water for cooking, and we also took this opportunity to wash ourselves and our dirty laundry. We had no soap, but a rinsing was better than nothing and felt refreshing.

I climbed the ridge next to the road and saw the most wonderful panorama of the surrounding mountains…ridge line after ridge line greying off into the distance. What a sense of freedom we had! On the top of our ridge was a meadow, and all around me lay a carpet of purple, blue, yellow, white, and scarlet wildflowers that were stirring with the activity of several species of colorful butterflies. I considered myself fortunate to witness such a dazzling display.

Todd and Susie joined me on the ridge to experience the rewarding panorama and said that they had found a terrific campsite around the bend in the road. We wasted no time in moving our packs to the site. It was great, secluded under trees yet accessible to the Lolo Trail and water, and while Todd and Susie put up the tent, I chose a spot for hanging food and strung the necessary rope. Todd and Susie decided to nap for a while, and I sat on my foam pad and eventually napped in the sun on the point in front of our campsite. Dinner was at 6:00 p.m., about thirty minutes after we woke. Pasta Roma, peas, and ice cream (all freeze dried) was the choice.

After our meal, it was my turn to hang the food bag, so it wouldn't be raided by animals. I hiked down to the spot at the bottom of the hill where I had prepped the line earlier in the day. While I was hanging the food, I noticed a most interesting sight, one that filled me with both surprise and amazement. There—on the top of the ridge where I had seen all the butterflies—was the form of a person cloaked in robes. Now, this was not one of those visions where you think you see a person out of the corner of your eye, and, upon looking closer, turns out to be a cardboard box underneath a lamppost. This was different. The more I looked, the more I was convinced it was a robed figure. The figure had to be at least twenty-five feet tall, and it startled me when I first saw it. There it stood with the right hand held higher than the left, almost in a benediction stance.

After continued scrutiny and inspection, I decided to head up the hill to investigate. It was only after climbing about one third of the way up the hill that the form changed, and I discovered the figure to be a dead tree trunk, broken and scarred from a lightning strike in such a way as to give it the shape and coloration of a figure in robes. For some unknown reason my first impression was that it reminded me of those visions of Christ or Mary that people have claimed to see from time to time. Although I was raised in the Christian tradition, this struck me as unusual because I am not Catholic. When I was a child, my grandmother was Catholic, my mother was raised Presbyterian, my father dabbled in Buddhism, two of my parents' best friends were Jewish, and I ended up being confirmed as Lutheran. However, as I ventured forth into college and beyond, I can say that I had no strong ties to any one particular Christian doctrine or denomination. Still, this image stuck in my mind and impressed me as being a link to those times that we have had of feeling protected and cared for by a higher power. As I returned to the bottom of the hill to finish hanging the food, I discovered that figure was only visible from that particular location. Several steps to the left or the right altered the view enough that it no longer looked like a person. I returned to our tent for the evening, now believing more than ever that we had an unseen partner on this expedition. If we hadn't realized it earlier, this was the slap on the forehead I needed. It was as if God were saying, "Hello! I am with you. Do you understand that?"

Having had this experience, I found it amazing that I had so quickly created a religious image out of the form of a dead tree. What made my mind operate in this manner? Was it based on imagery that was ingrained into my brain as a child? Was it a random association, or was I maneuvered into the correct line of sight and influenced by God? I know that I would not be writing these words were it not for the powerful visual impact from this experience. We have spent much of our time worrying, despite the fact that we have had reminders along our journey that suggested we were being assisted and protected. I guess our angels or God wanted to make sure we got the point. Well, it worked! I got it!

This whole imagery issue has me deep in thought. What does our Creator look like? Why do we look the way we do? Some beliefs state that man was created in God's image, and I use the word "God" with no specific, religious, or denominational reference. If so, does it mean that we, therefore, resemble God in physical appearance? If one ponders the human body, it is interesting to note how this incredible machine is perfectly adapted to our life...on Earth. Every part and physical quality of the body, our height, weight, arms, legs, mouths, skin color, fingers, etc., is designed to maintain our existence and reproduction on this planet. But what need of existence on this specific planet, or any other for that matter, might an omnipotent, creative entity have? If God is infinite, universal, and everlasting, then the part of us that is in the likeness of God must have the same qualities. Looking inward to the intangible, one sees that the soul, our spirit, is the only part of us not bound to the laws of nature, as we understand them to be. Perhaps it may be more correct to say that we are created in God's spiritual image. Our feelings, capacity for compassion, trust, faith, love, and empathy are our infinite qualities and our direct links with the power and essence of the Creator. We would do well to look to them for guidance more often.

The reverse would also apply. Since we assume that God is a spiritual force, everlasting, infinite, and universal, there would be no need for a physical body which is limiting through its specialization. Perhaps spiritual entities, angels and the like take human form only to be understood by men and women. In this manner, people may more easily accept the presence of God, and God can work in the intangible.

Given our acceptance of a universal creative force, what might be the nature of our relationship with it? Does it renew itself? Most of us at one point have heard of and studied the water system. It's a closed system that operates on its own. Water falls from clouds as raindrops. The rain runs off of the land into rivers, seas, and oceans. Water evaporates into the air and eventually condenses as water vapor to form clouds, which will, in turn, provide more rain. This cycle occurs continually and can teach us much about that which is eternal in us. If part of our Creator is in us, then we are part of a greater power. To know the Creator, we can look inside ourselves. Just as a raindrop shares similarities with the ocean or the cloud from which it came, so do we carry an essence with us that is like God, only smaller. In keeping with this analogy, as individuals we may be more like snowflakes, each having differences yet fundamentally identical in composition. Eventually, we will return to the great pool from which we came and come to share full peace and knowledge. We study the small to understand the large. Similarly, we should look at the eternal qualities within ourselves, such as love, to begin to know God.

Having philosophized for some length, I returned to this evening's events and plans. After dinner, Todd, Susie, and I got more water and settled in for the evening. We are excited by the trail, as far as Lewis and Clark sites are concerned, but we are finding the lack of water to be disturbing, even dangerous. This has made us have a change of plans, and we plan to be off the trail and back on Route 12 in two days. Our new plan for tomorrow is to hike to a site called Howard Camp, named after a general from the 1800s, because we know it's near a running stream. From there we will take Road #107 down to Route 12 where we will camp for the remaining 2.5 days while we wait for our support vehicle. Susie is finding the isolation slightly frightening, Todd's heels are in bad shape, and I am concerned about our health and safety. We should all feel better when we are off the Lolo Trail and Thursday arrives.

Hitchhiking in the Palm of God
July 18, 1994, Monday

We decided to come down early off the Lolo Trail due to the lack of water and the blisters on Todd's heels. The clouds made an attempt to threaten our good weather, but the sun eventually won out. Our backpack today took us four miles to the junction of 500 and 107. We never saw Devil's Chair, a large, natural rock formation, because there were no signs or trails visible to us as we hiked toward 107. Disappointed, but not surprised at the lack of signage and directions for historical sites and points of interest, we started our descent on 107, a dirt road. A road sign at the junction indicated that it was nine miles to Route 12. Bracing ourselves for the strain of the long downhill hike, during which we would descend 3,600 feet, we left the Lolo Trail and headed for Route 12 and, we thought, a telephone.

The hike down on 107 consisted of mostly switchbacks, and our toes ached from the continual jamming of our toes into the front of our boots. Todd did not want to stop because of his blistered heels; the sooner we reached the bottom, the sooner the boots could come off.

Susie has kept our minds occupied during much of our backpacking over the past few days by keeping us engaged in some interesting conversations. They were great fun and ranged from serious talks to lighter and sillier topics such as our favorite foods, movies, etc. Her energy seemed to make some of the more difficult times pass much faster.

Finally, the Lochsa River and Route 12 came into view, although the mile markers indicated that there were four miles to go. They were the longest four miles I've ever hiked, but eventually we rounded a bend in the road, and Route 12 lay before us.

We walked across the two lane road, which curved out of sight in both directions, and we headed down a dirt trail where we had lunch and used the opportunity to remove our boots. A campsite and a phone were our next priorities. We thought that if we could make it to the Lochsa Historical Ranger Station, our prearranged pick-up point, I could call our next Rig driver, and tell her that we were off the trail early. The only problem was that the Ranger Station was 18 miles west of our present location. After searching the area for suitable campsites, we decided to try and find a ride west to the Lochsa Historical Ranger Station. It was 2:00 p.m. at this point.

Finding no one to ask for a ride, we did the next best thing; we hitched. This seemed uncomfortable to me, since I would never dream of doing this in New Jersey, but somehow in the middle of a forest in Idaho it seemed safe, especially since all three of us were together. We must have presented a pretty disheveled sight for passing motorists, of which there were precious few. To make a long story short, we stood, sat, and lay on the side of the road for one and a half hours. Todd took photos of Susie and me with our thumbs out as he lay in the weeds on the opposite side of the road. The people that did come down the road passed and waved, and one person turned his car around at our intersection of logging road 107 and Route 12.

Finally a small, blue car coming east, opposite from the direction we wanted to go, pulled over, and a young woman named Erin asked if we needed a ride. Enthusiastic, we said that we needed to go to the ranger station, and she invited us to pack ourselves and our packs into her compact car. It seems that Erin had passed us once and decided to turn around, come back, and offer us a ride. I sat in front holding Erin's computer, and Todd and Susie sat in the back seat with both of our packs on their laps. Susie's pack managed to fit into the trunk. Amidst our packs and Erin's belongings, we settled in, as she turned her car around and headed west on Route 12.

Now...I need to make this perfectly clear. "Fast" does not accurately describe Erin's driving, and all of us wished, hoped, and prayed that we would make it to our destination in one piece. Route 12, you see, is a very winding, rather narrow highway that follows the banks of the Lochsa River. With this in mind you can understand my (our) distress at Erin's fondness for pushing the speed on curves and passing, with a limited view, semi-trucks that were transporting logs. Erin, however, seemed very calm as she told us that she used to work in Lolo and that she was presently on her way home to Lewiston, Idaho, from college in Denver. She was also looking into graduate programs in psychology. As if the ride were not already exciting enough, Erin popped in a Counting Crows tape which seemed to fuel her confidence in driving the snake-like road. I confess that I had to put my sunglasses on to hide the fear in my eyes, praying with clenched, sweaty palms that we would live to see another day. Finally the ranger station came into view, and we thankfully unloaded ourselves and our packs. Erin gave us her address and phone number and invited us to stop in when we reached Lewiston, Idaho. We were very grateful for the ride but knew that we already had plans for other accommodations. Still, the fact was not lost on me that we had been provided with a ride when we really needed it. Our luck, fate, protective presence still seemed to be with us.

Anticipation built as we headed up the steps to the Lochsa station. Most of the site was a museum. We walked into the office and met Gail, a mature woman that worked as an interpreter. Unbelievably, there was no phone at the station. It seemed they used radios for all their communication, but Gail told us that the nearest phone was 40 miles east at the Powell Ranger Station or 24 miles west in Lowell, ID. My hopes of easily locating a phone were dashed, and we walked out feeling quite disappointed. The only good part of all of this was that we were at our meeting point for the Rig, and there was a campground one mile east up the road.

As we walked down the steps to the parking lot, a retired couple from Florida named Ellis and Marie Ware pulled in with their RV bus. We asked if they had a car phone, knowing that there probably wasn't an available service cell, even if they did. They said they did not but would be willing to make a call for me when they got to Lowell. I wrote a message for the Wares to give to our Rig driver, hoping it would not alarm her. It simply said that we were out early, but OK, and that she could pick us up earlier on Wednesday if it was convenient. If not, Thursday would still be fine. While I was talking to the Florida couple, Todd and Susie were playing with two puppies that were riding with a trucker from Montana. They were both Labrador retrievers, one black and one yellow, each about six months old. Before Marie and Ellis drove off, they asked all three of us if we would like a Coke. Checking with each other to see if we heard correctly, we jumped at the chance and politely accepted their offer—not believing that we would be drinking anything as extravagant as Coca Cola today after four days of little water or water that tasted like iodine due to our water purification system. Pulling out a storage compartment from the side of their deluxe RV, Ellis handed us each an ice cold can of Coke. We thanked them again, said good-bye, and returned to the steps leading up to the ranger station to savor our civilized beverage. I wondered, for a second, how much Lewis and Clark missed the little comforts of home when they were on their journey.

Well, after our Cokes were finished, we were in a much better and much sillier mood. We hiked our packs back to the Wilderness Gateway campsites and found a scenic spot by the river. The sites cost six dollars per night, but all we had on us were two dollar bills and a $100 traveler's check. This posed a problem for us because the exact dollar amount had to be placed in an envelope and deposited in a locked metal box via a letter slot. We decided to camp and talk the ranger into letting us pay on Wednesday when the RV and our cash arrived.

We built a campfire, as we had the night before, and went to sleep at 10:30 under a three-quarter moon.

July 19, 1994, Tuesday

This was quite a varied day for me. In the morning, we were entertained by the multitude of ground squirrels that live in the campground. Apparently they have been fed by other visitors, so they are quite brave and come very close to you. If you are not careful, they will go through your packs in search of food.

Bolstered by yesterday's experience, I decided after breakfast that I would try to hitch a ride into Lowell, Idaho, which is twenty-four miles west, in order to call and make sure our driver got the message from the Wares and was not worried. I started talking to some people around our campsite, hinting for a ride. I had an interesting conversation with a retired couple named Boyd and Nida Harrison from Lewiston, who were camped in their trailer across the road. They had been camping here at the Wilderness Gateway Campground for years, and I told them why we were here and all about the difficulties we had with water and trail markers. They told an interesting story about a man and woman that hiked out of this campground four years ago. They were staying five sites down from us and had decided to hike up on the ridge. What they did not expect was for their day to become a deadly lesson in following basic hiking guidelines.

It seems that they were following a trail and decided to abandon it, perhaps for water. One thing led to another, and they became disoriented and lost. They finally found a stream and decided to follow the streambed, hoping it would lead down to the Lochsa River and Route 12. Apparently it was a very grueling hike, so much so that, despite words of encouragement from the man, the woman reached a point of total exhaustion and collapsed beside a tree. Four days after they had left, campers spotted the man, most certainly dehydrated, totally exhausted, and perhaps in shock, crossing the Lochsa River and returning to camp alone. When he was met by others, he informed them that his companion was dead. The first rescue helicopter that was called refused to search for individuals if they were confirmed dead, so a second rescue helicopter was summoned from Granger. When they reached the body, they found that rigor mortis had "frozen" the woman's body in a sitting position, and they were unable to secure her body to the stretcher. They wondered how they would extricate her from the ridgeside location. After many long, sad hours at the Wilderness Gateway Campground, campers were given a shocking and macabre sight as a helicopter was finally spotted returning down the river valley, intending to land across the river from the campground where emergency vehicles were parked. Dangling from a rescue rope underneath the helicopter was the woman's body supported by a harness, still in the sitting position in which she died. There was not a dry eye in the campground, but there was a very hard lesson learned in the precautions that should be taken and followed when hiking in the wilderness.

This story was amazing to hear from people who had witnessed it, and, on a side note, proved even more timely because there are currently four people presumed lost in this forest. Two search helicopters flew over this morning. The lost people are two days late returning from their hike, and the only possible lead was from the pilot of a small plane that spotted four individuals hiking by a lake up in the thick forest.

After the story was finished, Boyd told me that he was going fishing and could give me a ride to the Lochsa Historical Ranger Station. I accepted, thinking it was a start and would at least get me out to Route 12. During our drive, I explained again that I was a teacher, what we were doing, and why I needed to call my family. Boyd told me how he used to hunt up on and around the Lolo Trail area when he was fourteen to nineteen years old. During one of the trips, he remembered spotting a very old and large set of wheels down in a ravine. He thought nothing of it at the time, but years later he spoke to someone who was searching for General Howard's lost cannon that supposedly had rolled off the trail as it was being transported and never recovered. Howard Camp, one of our campsites on the Lolo Trail was named after General Howard. Boyd told him about his sighting and was eager to go back and locate it; however, it was never found. It might have been destroyed or covered by debris. Given the way snow changes the terrain in northern Idaho and the length of time between Boyd's visits, it is quite possible that the search was in the wrong location. The possibility exists that General Howard's cannon, or the remains of it, is still waiting to be discovered by a sharp-eyed backpacker or hunter somewhere along the Lolo Trail in Idaho.

After I was dropped off at the ranger station, I decided to go up and ask Gail if she knew of anyone who was going west to Lowell. She said that she did not know of someone but would be willing to spread the word to visitors that came in and suggested that I wait at the bottom of the steps. Seeing that it was already 10:00 a.m., I decided to try my luck on the road.

Before I go on, let's be clear about the facts. I was in the middle of some pretty remote wilderness region. In addition, not much traffic was on Route 12 at this time of day anyway, so I was forced to wait for a while between cars that were traveling west. Mind you, with the exception of rinsing myself in the Lochsa River this morning, I had not showered in five days, so I both looked and smelled pretty awful to someone who was not in the same situation. It, therefore, goes without saying that I was not the most presentable prospect for a driver to pick up in my hiking attire. Nonetheless, I waited and persisted for about twenty minutes, hoping for a car to stop. One car passed…the driver didn't even look at me. A second car…not even a glance. The third driver looked at me, perhaps considering picking me up, but, again, he didn't even slow down, whizzing right past me. During this time, I heard Todd calling to me from somewhere up in the forest on the opposite side of the river across the road. Try as I might, I could not locate him, so I yelled hello and waved blindly toward the area from where his shouts were coming.

After twenty minutes of trying to get a ride, a blue Honda Accord with Montana plates being driven by a middle-aged man in a white shirt and blue tie pulled over. I went up to the open passenger window and asked if he was going to Lowell. The driver introduced himself as Craig, said he was going directly through Lowell on his way to Lewiston, and invited me to get in. A bit nervously, I opened the door and got in the front seat. Perfect! Craig's car was air conditioned, which felt wonderful after standing in the hot sun.

At this point, something miraculous occurred. As we pulled away from the side of the road, I began to mention how I was traveling the Lewis and Clark Trail, and, with that, Craig looked at me quizzically.

Uh-oh, I thought, just how crazy is this guy? Just what do serial killers look like?

"You look familiar…I…I know you," Craig finally said, shaking his right index finger at me.

"No, I don't think so," I replied. "I'm from New Jersey, and this is my first trip out west. Ever been to Jersey?"

"No, I haven't, but I'm certain I recognize you from someplace. I knew it the moment I saw you on the road."

"I don't see how," I said, becoming a bit more unsettled. "I have no ties to this area, and you've never been to New Jersey, so I don't see any possible way that you could know me, unless you read the papers."

"You're Gordon Ward. You were on TV, weren't you? I think I heard about you during my stay in Great Falls," he blurted suddenly after thinking about it for a bit.

I was absolutely speechless. Could it be? I remembered the spontaneous interview that we had done with a news crew on the sidewalks of Great Falls, MT, after riding into the town about a week before this. Things started to fall into place from then on. Craig recalled information that he could not have known otherwise such as our six hour, ten mile day's ordeal with the wind north of Fort Peck. He also said that a blond haired man on the sports section of the ABC news program had run the story. Yes, that was it!

Really, what are the odds of this? I was in the middle of nowhere, in an area of the country where I've never visited previously, looking extremely bedraggled, and hitching for a ride. Within twenty minutes, I not only get a ride, but I get it from someone who *happened* to know me! And it's not just someone who knows me, but it's a stranger who just *happened* to have his television on in the evening — the evening that our interview aired, which probably lasted two minutes after editing. Craig said he found it while flipping through channels and decided to watch it because it looked interesting. He then just *happened* to be passing the spot where I had my thumb out, twenty minutes after I started looking for a ride! If he had been a half hour earlier, he would have missed me…a bit later, and I may have given up. Plus, upon seeing me standing on the shoulder of the road, he recognizes me and decides to stop! I would bet anyone that I could stand on the side of a road in my own town for twenty minutes and not get a ride, yet here I was, a couple of thousand miles away from my home in a wilderness area where I've never been, and I get a ride, a ride from someone who knows me! It literally gives me chills just thinking about it.

After more of a formal introduction, the remainder of the ride was spent educating Craig about the Lewis and Clark expedition. He asked many questions and was extremely interested in learning more about it. As I sat in the car, my thoughts turned to whether this occurrence was due to luck, guardian angels, or additional intervention from God, our unseen partner and guide. I was convinced it was definitely the latter. The string of "coincidences" we've encountered had made it impossible to think otherwise.

When we finally arrived in Lowell, I thanked Craig for the ride and got out of his car feeling very fortunate for such a good experience. Except for Erin's ride the day before, I have never hitchhiked, nor wanted to. I found myself rating the cars that approached in relation to the types of people that might be driving them. I felt bad for judging people by the vehicles they drove but considered it my only means of screening the people in this necessary, yet risky, activity. I had no other option for getting to a phone, but at least I was half way through my hitching experience. I was in Lowell and had only to call home and make it back to the campground.

As Craig drove away, I was struck by the size of Lowell: three buildings, which I could see, on the northern side of Route 12. One was a motel, the second was a diner/restaurant, and the third was a combination souvenir/service station/food store. My eye was then drawn to a sign that read "Welcome to Lowell. Population 24 23." Wow! Talk about your small towns! This had to be one of the smallest I had seen, and it looked like an interesting stop.

I headed for the restaurant called the Wilderness Inn. The AT&T sticker on the door satisfied my question about the telephone availability. Sure enough, just inside the door was a phone, and I wasted no time dialing home. The call went through, and I was hoping that someone would be home, since it was 2:30 p.m. in New Jersey. I was in luck. An agreement was made where to meet us with the Rig, and I also spoke to my daughter Melina, who was excited to leave soon to see me and wanted to know if I had any funny stories to tell.

After hanging up the phone at 11:45 a.m., my eye was drawn to the counter and the menu. I asked if they could cash a traveler's check, which they could, and I ordered a hamburger, fries, and a piece of coconut custard pie. They served some of the largest portions that I have ever seen, and it tasted like heaven after four days of freeze dried camping food. A television was turned on above the counter, and I noted that the television station was broadcasting from Denver, Colorado. One of the stories was about today being the twenty-fifth anniversary of the first moon walk, and I was reminded of my friend Dayton Duncan's comparison of the Lewis and Clark expedition to the space program; each was exploring the current frontier for our country. After finishing my pie, I thought it would be nice to surprise Susie and Todd with some "real" food. I ordered two cheeseburgers and two pieces of apple pie to go, waited for my order, paid at the counter, and walked to the other side of Route 12 to try my luck at getting a ride back to the campground.

I don't think that more than half a dozen cars went by before a blue Toyota 4x4 truck pulled over with a mountain bike attached to the roof. A young guy in sunglasses said that he was pulling in to get a sandwich at the Wilderness Inn but was willing to give me a ride if I wanted to wait. In the meantime, I was free to try my luck on the road. As he pulled into the parking lot, I decided not to push my luck any further and walked back to wait for my ride by the truck. I felt I was again being cared for and watched over, and could sense that taking this ride was the right thing for me to do.

A few minutes later the driver came out, introduced himself as Mike, and we pulled out heading east. Mike said that he was a recent college graduate working for the Nez Perce National Forest. He is an avid cyclist, hiker, and kayaker, and we hit it off very well. His degree is in botany, and I mentioned that my father used to be a botany professor at Fairleigh Dickinson University in Madison, NJ. Mike was also extremely interested in the Quest West trip. During our discussions, I asked Mike what he was doing over the summer, and he said that he was working with someone who had a Ph.D. in botany. They formed a team along with nineteen others to ground truth the satellite pictures of foliage in the forest. Basically they went out into the forest and recorded the types of trees and shrubs that were in different quadrants of the forest photos. In this way, scientists could learn to correlate different colors on the satellite photos with specific tree species. Very interesting! We discussed fire policy and how the National Parks were slowly starting to see the value of fires in the natural progression of the forest and other environments.

Mike was a free spirit who had experience riding 1,200 mile bike tours and hitchhiking throughout Canada and the U.S. He said he almost always picked up people that wanted a ride because of his own experiences. Mike insisted on driving me into the camp loop road, and, amidst final comments about fire policies and benefits, I again appreciated my good fortune in having had two excellent drivers and in making it back with lunch for Todd and Susie by 12:45 p.m. As Mike drove away, it dawned on me that all of the drivers who helped us out drove blue vehicles. The couple who gave us water, Erin, and Craig had blue cars, and Mike's truck was blue. Subconsciously, maybe this was one of the reasons I decided to wait for Mike at the Wilderness Inn. It just seemed too much of a common thread to chalk up to chance.

When I got back to our campsite, Todd and Susie were on a walk and returned at about 1:20 p.m., ready for lunch but expecting to have PB&J on pita bread. They were interested in finding out what had happened to me, but they were even more surprised when I pulled out the bags of cheeseburgers and pie after tantalizing them with the story of my lunch.

The river here is really beautiful, and I spent most of the afternoon exploring amidst the water and rocks while my satisfied companions napped under the tent's rain sheet. Later, while returning from a water refill, Nida Harrison called me into their campsite and asked me if I liked fish. When I said I did, Boyd came out of his RV with two frozen cutthroat trout that he had caught that morning on the Lochsa River. He said that he had plenty, and we were welcome to them if we wanted. This seemed too good to be true, but I gratefully accepted the trout and returned to camp with looks of amazement on Todd's and Susie's faces. Mine showed the same amazed expression, I'm sure.

One of our campground hosts has given us a hard time about not having money to pay for the campsite, despite our explanations about how this was an unforeseen twist in our plans and that the RV, which would be here on Wednesday or Thursday, would have the correct amount of money. We would definitely pay at that point. While in Lowell, I was able to cash the traveler's check but was so intent on talking to my family and getting lunch that correct change for the campground completely slipped my mind.

Anyway, as I went to get water with Todd after dinner, we passed the hosts, a man and a woman. The woman had earlier mentioned the rangers OK to our situation, but I guess the gentleman felt like he had to say something. He reminded us that we were against regulations because we should have paid one half hour after choosing our site. He also indicated that he did not think we intended to pay. This upset me since he was now attacking our character; however, we told him that we were honest people, and the campground would get their money. I even offered to pay him with a $20.00 bill if he could give us change. His response was that the money had to be put in the box. I left, thinking of how to respond to the situation.

As far as I was concerned, if the ranger had given the OK, these confrontations were not necessary, yet our hosts were making me uncomfortable. I decided to go to other campsites to try and find change for my $20.00 bill. This would allow us to register and put this situation behind us. No one to whom I spoke could help, but on my return trip to our site, Nida called me over to their campsite once again where she was playing scrabble with Boyd. They offered to help me out with correct change, and I was able to exchange my $20.00 bill for three "fives" and five "ones"...another unrequested provision from God. I knew that I could now pay the exact amount and did so promptly in order to silence our hosts.

On the way back to our campsite, I asked the Harrisons for their recommendations on cooking trout. Nida asked me if we had a pan, to which I had to admit we did not. As soon as I admitted this, Boyd came out of his RV with a large, black, cast iron skillet and said that it would do the trick. Accepting graciously, I was then asked if we had bread crumbs. Before I could answer completely, Boyd invited me into their RV for "fixings." He gave me a small baggie full of bread crumbs and a container of vegetable oil to put in the pan for cooking. I left feeling extremely grateful and a little embarrassed of how much Nida and Boyd had done for us. They have both been a huge help to us over the past two days, angels on Earth, if you will.

Time after time, we found ourselves being provided with the things we needed on this trip. Some may have been literally life-saving provisions. No longer did I feel these events to be luck or coincidences. We were, I'm quite sure, in the presence of angels, accompanied by a divine presence, and quite literally hiking—even hitchhiking—in the presence of God, as we all are every second of our lives. We had seen nine faces of God, nine occurrences when God revealed Himself and His grace through events, people, and angels: the storm, the road grader, the couple who gave us water on the trail, the vision of the robed figure on the hill, Erin, Craig, Mike, Ellis and Marie Ware, and Boyd and Nida Harrison. Whoever thinks miracles don't happen need to take a closer look at their lives and consider that God and angels are still very much at work and very present in our lives. Perhaps it is us who need to open our eyes and our minds, acknowledge the divine influences in our lives, and watch for the miracles to happen.

our minds, acknowledge the divine influences in our lives, and watch for the miracles to happen.

Considering Connections, Awareness, and Divine Immersion

The whole of life swirls in spirals and eddies around us from the moment we take our first breath to the time we transcend this earth. Events come and go. Sights and sounds dance before our eyes and demand our attention, even compete for our attention, so that, sometimes, it's hard to say for sure what our present reality is. At times it appears as if we are in control of our lives, but then, in an instant, we can be thrown into a frenzy, the very ground shifting beneath our feet, and we realize, we have lost all control.

The truth is, we never really have control of anything. Oh, we're pretty good at predicting outcomes. If one were placing bets, there are certain things that are easier to predict with accuracy than others, but even these "certainties" are really just situations that have the odds stacked in their favor. Underneath everything is the ever-present hum of unpredictability.

However, there is a continuity that holds our lives together. There is a web that connects everything to everything else. Sometimes these connections are very apparent, and other times they are elusive as vapors. If we're lucky, there are opportunities for us to see the connections between the events in our lives. Often, they take generations to reveal themselves. The trick to identifying them is to expand one's awareness. This can be difficult to do in today's hectic world, but it is possible if one starts small. Begin with remembering more of the simple things you do in your life. Run them over in your mind. Ruminate on them. In time, you'll be able to remember more of what you do each day, and with this expanded memory will come a greater awareness of your life and the ways in which it transects the lives of others. Eventually, you'll see a clearer cause and effect relationship begin to reveal itself in your life.

I no longer believe in coincidences. I think that our Creator has a plan for us—all of us—and those plans include a great deal of learning that we need to accomplish. I prefer to call coincidences "Godincidences," those moments when it seems like there is no way on Earth that things could have worked out the way they have without some higher-level guidance or pre-direction. We've all had them. The events I describe in "The Nine Faces of God," for example, fit this bill to a tee. Godincidences leave us amazed, astonished, and at an utter loss for words to describe why they happened as they did.

I have to admit that my trip along the Lewis and Clark Trail changed my life completely. Experience has shown me that there is a God that takes care of us. When I was retracing the route of Lewis and Clark, one of the parts that excited me the most was the promise of canoeing along the "wild and scenic" portion of the Missouri River in Montana. This was the time when we would be on the river itself, in the same fashion that Lewis and Clark traveled, and camping in places where they camped.

One day after getting on the river, I got sick...really sick. It was all I could do to crawl out of the canoe at the end of the day, pull myself up on the shore, and lay on the bank. I was nauseous with a fever, and I couldn't stand up easily due the dizziness I was experiencing. The next day, Todd had to paddle me out to a waiting van. Two days later in Great Falls, at the second hospital I visited, I was finally diagnosed with Lyme disease— the first known case of the disease in the state, according to my doctors. I was bitten by a tick in New Jersey two weeks earlier but didn't experience any symptoms until I was in Montana.

At the time, I was angry. I had looked forward to that segment of the trip for a year. It was one of the pinnacles of our trip, and I missed a good portion of the experience because I was flat on my back. With time, however, I came to realize that, if I had to get Lyme disease, this point of the trip was the only time when Todd could get me to safety under his own power. If I had been stricken while riding on the open rangeland of Montana, out of contact with civilization, Todd would not have been able to peddle me out to a hospital. If I had become sick during the days we were backpacking on the Lolo Trail in Idaho, Todd certainly couldn't have carried me out for treatment. The river, when we were in a canoe, was the only time he could get me to medical treatment under his own power. In the end, getting sick on the river was actually the best scenario, the best time for me to have become ill.

Often we get too caught up in labeling events as good or bad. I think that limits us. Instead, what if there weren't good or bad? Oh, sure, there are certainly joyous and sad events that take place in our lives. But does joyous and sad translate to good and bad? Not necessarily. Take, for example, the subject of kidnapping. Is it good or bad? Most people would deem it bad, but let's take a closer look.

Few people know that there was a woman named Watkuweis who saved the lives of Lewis and Clark and the rest of the men on the exploration. When the men stumbled, half dead after crossing the snow-laden Rocky Mountains, into the village of the Nez Percé, they were welcomed by the tribe. That evening, however, unbeknownst to Lewis and Clark, the village took a vote to kill Lewis and Clark and the rest of the men, largely because their guns, ammunition, trade beads, and other supplies would have made them the most powerful and richest tribe west of the Rocky Mountains. Only one, old, Nez Percé woman, Watkuweis, stood up and said no, and the tribe agreed not to kill the men. Why did she disagree with her tribe? Because, when she was a little girl, Watkuweis was kidnapped from the Nez Percé and eventually found herself living with a white family on the west coast. This white family treated her very well, much like they would have treated their own daughter. Eventually, when she was older, Watkuweis was able to make her way back to her native Nez Perćé tribe. When the time came to decide the fate of Lewis and Clark, Watkuweis explained to her village, "The white people were good to me when I was young. Now it is our time to return that favor."

So, was the kidnapping of Watkuweis good or bad? Well, I imagine it was certainly sad when it occurred, and it was probably deemed to be bad. But, given time, it turned out to have a purpose, an amazing purpose. Watkuweis was treated well by her white family, she made it back to her people, and her experience was the only thing that saved the Lewis and Clark party. Without that kidnapping, the men would have disappeared in the mountains. Talk about a Godincident! That one was pretty amazing.

Still not convinced? Did you know that Lewis and Clark took a sixteen-year-old Mandan woman with them who had just given birth to a baby boy? Many of you will know this is true and that her name was Sacagawea. During the first winter of the exploration, Meriwether Lewis met Sacagawea when he was asked by the Mandan village to treat her during her particularly hard labor. He mixed dried, powdered rattles from a rattlesnake into a solution and gave it to her. Several minutes later, Sacagawea delivered her baby. During this time, it was discovered that she spoke Shoshone. This, the explorers knew, would be extremely helpful because the men would need to acquire horses from this tribe to get over the Rocky Mountains. As a result, it was arranged for her to accompany them, along with her French husband.

Sacagawea proved to be very helpful to the exploration. She saved some of the journals that Lewis and Clark had written by jumping into the river and retrieving them after they were washed overboard in some rough water. She and her baby served as a peace symbol on the journey because war parties don't carry women with infants. Sacagawea helped the exploration by recognizing landforms as the group traveled west. Most importantly, however, Sacagawea not only helped with the interpretation with the Shoshone, she just about guaranteed that Lewis and Clark would get all the horses they needed for their mountain crossing. Why? Because, unbeknownst to anyone, Sacagawea ended up being the sister of the Shoshone chief. How did this happen? Sacagawea was kidnapped from the Shoshone tribe when she was a young girl and sold to the Mandan Indians where Lewis and Clark discovered her some eight years later. What are the chances that she would have needed their help with her labor during that winter of 1804-1805? What are the chances that Lewis and Clark, unknowingly, would meet and want to take with them the only Mandan woman who could have guaranteed their success with the Shoshone tribe? The odds are absolutely astronomical. It was a historic Godincident.

Was it divine intervention? I wouldn't exactly put it in those words. I prefer not to think that God intervenes in our lives. To me, the term "divine intervention" conjures up an image of an omniscient being who stands back, letting us flounder on our own, only to jump in to save the day at the last possible moment. I don't think it works like that. I believe, instead, in "divine immersion," meaning that we are saturated in a divine presence every second we live. Our Creator is always with us, guiding us, caring for us. Sometimes, like any parent knows, things are going to hurt and seem unfair, even if they are for the best. It's at those times in our lives, when we can't see the purpose or the reason for things that cause us pain or sadness, that we have to trust that we are still immersed in God's care and His special plans for us as individuals. All things, even the challenging and painful parts of life serve a purpose, so we have to be careful with the way we label events.

When we label things or events as good or bad, I think it's akin to putting one's nose on a stained-glass window and judging what it seen. If this were to happen, you would see shapes and colors, but they wouldn't have any relationship or continuity. You would declare some shapes or colors as strange, ugly, or unnecessary…or good or bad based solely upon a limited point of view. It's only after stepping back from the window and viewing it from afar with a different perspective, that one would be able to see the entire image. You would see how those shapes and colors, which you once deemed strange, ugly, or unnecessary, fit into the entire picture. Without them, the image in the window would be incomplete.

Even the worst events can be turned around within God's plan. Consider the crucifixion of Jesus in terms of the way it has been viewed over time. The disciples initially saw this as the worst thing that could have ever happened. They feared for their lives. They hid themselves away in a secret room. As far as they knew, their leader had been executed, and they were scared that they might be next. Nothing good could ever come from this, they thought. But Christians today view the crucifixion and the resurrection as the best thing that ever happened to the world. Out of the darkness of a brutal, Roman execution came the salvation of mankind.

Try to allow the terms "good" and "bad" to fade and consider that time may cast a different perspective on events in your life. This isn't always easy. Applying and embracing this response to life involves trust, security, liberation, responsibility, and a sense of purpose. We need to trust that God is caring for us, every day and every second. We need to trust that there is a plan designed just for us. If we do this, we can find great security in knowing God's arms are always holding us. Security, in turn, breeds liberation, an incredible sense of freedom that comes from knowing we are following a path laid out for us by a loving, eternal Creator. We are part of a much grander picture. However, the flipside of liberation is responsibility. We are here to accomplish a desired set of deeds and goals that God has set before us, so this demands that we be responsible for our actions. We need to uphold our role in the divine, stained glass window of existence. Life has many storms that can divert the directions and courses of our lives, but we all have important roles to fulfill. If we continue to be mindful of this, life takes on a beautiful, new sense of purpose. We may not be able to see over the horizon, but we have a direction in which to sail, and we know we will never be alone. Even when it seems we have lost our way, we can rest in the knowledge that we have guides, are we are never alone.

My hope is that we will all take more time to climb out of our own skin and contemplate how events may affect the future, rather than just ourselves. Let us take the time to expand our awareness. Let us take the time to consider that events affect more than just our lives. Let us think about the grand scope of future events and how our universe's eternal, creative force connects the past with the present and the future. Let us trust and wallow in our divine immersion.

Chapter 3
All Beautiful the March of Days

Initium Novum

Her eyes were like winter. They mirrored the early, brittle morning—haunting, evocative, and peaceful, but as dark and cold as iron. Surrounding us, the grasses of the Great Swamp stood coated in frost, yearning for the coming warmth of sunrise, but the frigid breeze stifled their prayers for warmth, echoed in the clicking of the grey branches overhead. The whole world seemed to be holding its breath, waiting for deliverance. I was in the middle of my morning run, following the gravel road in the growing light, when I head a rustling at my side. Somewhat startled and turning, I saw a young doe, just growing out of her fawn stage, standing three feet to my left, her white, camouflage spots still scattered like large flakes of snow on her hips. She was chewing the grass she had found along the side of the road, and, due to her youth and inexperience, had not yet learned the fear of man. Needless to say, I stopped running, surprised by this close encounter, and stared into her eyes, and there we stood—me watching her watching me—and all was hushed and still under the growing light of that new day and soon-to-be new year.

Have you ever been entranced by innocence? Maybe you've encountered it with a newborn baby, a child, or an animal. It changes your outlook and perceptions in an instant, as it did for me that frozen morning. It heralds a new beginning, an *initium novum*. There I was in my microfiber and fleece and, until that moment, deep in thought about my upcoming day's responsibilities, until I was utterly derailed by the gaze of this animal. There was simplicity and trust in her eyes, and somewhere in that scene was also a sense of reassurance, a promise that our needs would be met. There, on that roadside in a national wildlife refuge, was evidence that innocence and simplicity are not overlooked in this world by our creator. Oh, sure, it's easy to get distracted and feel like we are apart or, worse yet, above nature, but when we distill life down to its foundation, we find there is God and there is everything else, His creation.

It's moments like these that remind us how intertwined we are in God's masterpiece. We are all, each one of us, a part of the mixture of life, a component of the beautiful wholeness of this world. Mine was a grounding, humbling moment. Here was this almost defenseless young deer, seemingly alone in the dark and the cold, and the God of the universe was providing for her needs, giving her sustenance and unexpected company in the form of me, someone who should have been viewed by the doe as a natural predator, someone who had set out seeking solitude and rejuvenation without any thought of creation or communion. It was a moment I came very close to missing, but benevolence and awareness made it a blessed gift.

What can we learn from this? What does this mean going forward? Behold, God is doing a new thing every second! Perceive it. Behold this *initium novum*, this new beginning! Let it overtake you, fill you, engulf you. Embrace it as an opportunity of grace. It's a chance to realign one's feelings and thoughts. It's an opportunity to let go of perceptions and behaviors and memories that are holding us back. It's a time to believe that God has an amazing plan for us all. It's a time to trust our Creator, experience new things, stretch our imaginations, and remember that infinite grace abounds for not only us but for all of God's creation. Remember to embrace innocence. Remember that we are not as independent as we think we are. Remember that we all are part of everything that surrounds us. Deer, runners, frozen grass and trees, business people, teachers, ministers, and anything else you can imagine are part of the divine recipe. Seek to emulate the young doe in the Great Swamp, singular yet a beloved part of the amalgamation of life, and rest in the knowledge that God knows you and will provide for you in ways you cannot even begin to imagine.

January may be a customary time for annual reflection, but the messages here are ones that ring just as true and clear at any other time or day of the year. Don't miss a thing! Embrace the possibilities, hold fast to your faith, trust that you are living in the lap of God, and live every second as a gifted, new beginning — your *initium novum*.

Perfect Fractures

I have always believed that if one really loves something, one should be willing to see it through all kinds of weather. This goes for people as well as places, but in this case, I'm referring to a particular location. There is a lovely, historic place in Bernardsville along Hardscrabble Road that is my spiritual sanctuary. Owned by the Audubon Society and the National Park Service, it is a place where I go to recharge. The trails are frequented by many hikers on sunny, warm days, but the woods are empty when the weather turns inclement, and I often wonder why people aren't more curious about the changes that overtake the area during these times. What can be seen that's new? What sights might be discovered?

On the evening of January 16, 2009, my friend Joe and I set off on a hike. Despite the temperature being four degrees, we wanted to experience this place we knew so well while it was frozen. We were told there was something wrong with us, that our minds must have snapped to want to go out in that weather, but we were undeterred. We departed from our homes and families and drove out to the wintered woods. Dressed for the weather, fractured minds or not, we set out under the cover of darkness on this moonless evening to see what lies hidden to most people.

Arriving at the trailhead, we stepped off the road and into the snow.

"Turn off your headlamp," I said to Joe. "Let's try to do this with the available light."

We did. It didn't take long before our eyes adjusted, and we saw the world around us transformed. The mantle of white snow acted as a perfect backdrop, contrasting the trunk of every tree and the contours of every rock. It was so cold that the crystalline snow squeaked and crunched under our feet. A light breeze bit at our exposed faces as we trudged ahead, gradually beginning to feel part of our surroundings.

We stopped at a hearth built by the New Jersey Brigade in December 1779, and I reminded Joe that the soldiers that camped here saw temperatures rise above zero only once in January 1780. The cold we were feeling through our four layers of modern, insulating clothing was the high temperature for the entire month with four feet of standing snow on the ground, and they had only rags to wear. We had no reason to complain, and soon, feeling embarrassed for even thinking about the cold in the proximity of this place of personal sacrifice, we moved on up the hill.

Blazing our own trail, we climbed up the slope, navigating over fallen trees and around large boulders. Twice we stopped, took off our hoods, and listened; listened to the sound of the frozen night, listened to the dead Ironwood leaves rustle in the frigid breeze as they clung to their skeletal branches, listened to the sound of our own breaths, listened to the tree limbs crackling over our heads, listened to the deep sound of nightfall embracing the hilltop. We were the only ones standing in the woods, but there was another presence in our midst. We could both sense it, something wonderful, something protective, mysterious, natural, and reassuring.

After several minutes our ears began to sting, so we pulled our hoods over our heads and headed down to the stream that forms the beginning of the Passaic River. There, the sounds of babbling water mixed with the occasional cracking of ice, punctuated by our own footfalls in the crusted snow.

Arriving at a flat area on the bank, we stopped to drink some hot tea we had brought with us in thermoses. I don't know what possessed me, but I suddenly dropped my pack and lay down on my back in the snow and looked straight up.

"Joe," I whispered, "you have to see this. Try it."

He did, and we both lay there, several yards apart and with different perspectives, marveling at the magical view above our heads. One particularly gnarled tree stretched its jet black branches above us, the branch tips mixing with those of the trees around it. Above this was a clear, blue-black sky scattered with silver, winking stars. When we squinted our eyes, it appeared as if the sky was fractured, the branches looking like spidery cracks extending across the sky.

"It looks like ice," said Joe.

"It mirrors the ice on the river," I responded, our breaths ascending into the night sky.

No description or photograph could ever do justice to the view we had before our eyes, and we marveled at this gift of nature that God had fashioned. It was then that I knew what we felt in the woods. The very designer of the stars in the heavens and the architect of our natural world walked with us that night—a sublime and silent partner. The gift was above us, and its creator was with us the whole time we were hiking, waiting for us to look up and see.

We lay there in the frozen powder for several minutes, neither of us saying a word, transfixed by the scene: a river in darkness, covered with fractured ice, running beside fractured men under a fractured sky, created by a perfection that treasures and loves us all...regardless of the weather in our lives.

God's Transitions

Stepping through the door into the early morning air, I expected to be hit with the usual, late winter chill. With dawn just about to break, hands in the pockets of my insulated coat, and head held low, I was prepared for the biting cold. It never came. Instead, change was in the air, having slipped in unannounced and undetected overnight. There was a slight softness to the breeze, and a sense that was almost hopeful permeated the more temperate emergent light. I smiled. "There it is," I thought, "that redemptive, first sign of spring."

The change of seasons is an event that is never lost on me. It's actually one of the reasons why I continue to live in the northeast. I find it to be a balm, a source of nourishment for my spirit. Every seasonal transition carries its own trials and pleasures, but it is the winter to spring transition that carries the most promise — promise of gentler weather, promise of new growth, and the hope that the snows, which seemed so magical in December but had since grown dreary and tiresome, have departed for another nine months. There was almost a palpable sense of celebration in the air and a release of tension born of several months of resistance to the assaulting cold of winter.

I wondered if everyone was attuned to this first breath of spring, the first blush of rebirth. Are we all aware of it, or do some people, those who remain too sheltered or hidden from their environment, completely miss this seasonal annunciation? There is something visceral and instinctive involved in noticing the seasonal changes, and I welcome the experiences. Not only do I look forward to the changes, I treasure the way in which they make their presence known, often in a very subtle and gradual manner.

I think God sometimes works in much the same manner, His work and approach often reflected in the seasons. When God whispers in our ears, are we aware of His messages, those soft tugs at our consciences, the divine vapors that urge our minds to pursue particular actions? Do we always notice them, and, if so, do we heed them?

These hallowed messages don't follow the same rhythm as the changes of the seasons, but they surely occur. In fact, they occur with greater regularity, as often as the sun rises, indeed, as often as we draw our breaths! Change is often resisted, but it is God's will playing out in our lives. It is the very bedrock of creation. Welcome it. Embrace it. Expect it every moment that you live. Open yourself up to the simple miracle of God's changes upon your hearts and minds. Allow your souls to ring like bells in a choir. Inhale His will for you and fulfill your part in His grand rhapsody of life.

God reveals His wisdom every day. Remind yourself, as I often do for myself, of this essential truth. As the lengthening daylight of springtime fills our lives, think about the ways that God illuminates your world more and more with each passing day. May we all step out of our doors every morning—out of our shells—with an awareness, an acceptance, and a deep appreciation for God's transitions in our lives. Breathe in God. Feel the soft, gentle wind of hope embodied in this new season and greet the emergent zephyrs of God that blow through your soul.

Blooming for God

March brings spring, a time of rebirth in our annual cycle, but for *Tahina spectabilis*, March may not be any more significant than any other time of the year. Do you know what *Tahina spectabilis* is? If not, that's okay because no one else knew until mid-January of 2008. It is a brand new species of palm tree that was discovered in Madagascar. This tree blooms only once after approximately one hundred years of life, and then it dies. No doubt, this discovery will be discussed at great length in botany circles, but I think it's relevant to discuss in this forum as well. The things that caught my attention were the similarities this tree has to people and the lessons it can teach us.

This tree has a life span very similar to ours.

It continues to grow throughout its life.

When it reaches a certain maturity, it is capable of providing shelter and support for other species.

It seeks to establish a firm root base capable of weathering many storms.

When it is not blooming, it looks much like other species of palms.

However, the major characteristic that makes this tree different from others is also the quality that can teach us the most. This tree blooms just once. It literally blooms itself to death by devoting so much energy into this single event. As humans, we get the chance to bloom every second we breathe. We live and grow and interact with others, with each moment presenting itself as an opportunity to shine and show our colors — to live a life consistent with our faiths. Most often, we lose track of these opportunities because we say, "Well, there's always tomorrow." But how do we know? What if we were given only one chance to bloom? What if that chance is right now? How would that change the way we live and the way we treat each other? What if, instead of viewing our lives as a series of chances, we viewed each of our life spans as one, singular, extended, blooming season? The results would be spectacular.

We only live once on this planet. Unlike *Tahina spectabilis*, we bloom continuously over the course of approximately one hundred years. Let's not waste our moments in the sun. Let us make the most of our time on Earth and literally bloom ourselves out for God.

The Unexpected

I remember an unusually warm day we had one March when the temperature actually hit eighty degrees. Ahh! Spring has finally arrived, I thought. Many people busied themselves with tidying yards, going for walks, opening windows, and even taking the convertible out for a spin. The whole world seemed to be letting out a huge sigh of relief.

As I wrote this three days later, I was catching up from being late to my office because I had to scrape two inches of snow off of my car, deal with unpredictable road conditions, and anticipate the even more capricious behaviors of other drivers. I was wondering at the time if there was anyone else who thought maybe, just maybe, we were finished with snow for the winter and that relief had arrived? That snow wasn't even in the forecast! Was I the only one lulled into a false sense of security from our early brush with springtime?

Then, as my mind was begrudging the fact that I once again had to worry about skidding on the roads, I caught myself actually admiring the snow-covered trees along Tempe Wick Road in Mendham and New Vernon, NJ. They were stunning with their white frosting. The top and windward side of each and every trunk, branch, and twig was adorned with snow and contrasted against the dark grey bark, which was visible on their leeward sides. I thought of stopping to capture the scene in a photograph, but I decided against doing so. It wouldn't translate or be anywhere near as impressive on camera. This was God's canvas presenting an image that was viewed very much by the heart.

Often, God throws us curveballs. We are presented with the unexpected all the time; yet, we are always surprised by it, and, often, it frustrates us. After all, we had *our* plans. We had *our* expectations. It's difficult to relinquish our feelings of vexation and look at the opportunities that reside within the unexpected, but it's worth the effort.

As spring arrives, I'm going to try to see what lies beneath the shell of surprise, and I'd like to invite you to try to discover it with me. The unexpected dashes our plans and forces an altered perspective, but it also offers gifts of insight that we wouldn't have had otherwise. Whether it's the surprise of morning snow in New Vernon in 2011 or the discovery of an empty tomb in Jerusalem in the year 33, the unexpected awaits. God has a new direction to take us. We just have to be willing to let our hearts and minds follow him on the journey, which presents, for many, the ultimate reward and the ultimate challenge.

Wake Up!

I don't like alarms...not one bit. No matter when I set my alarm to go off, I always wake up beforehand. If it's set for 7:00 a.m., I wake up at 5:45, 6:20, 6:50, over and over again, just so I won't have to hear that intrusive alarm. I do this because I don't like to be startled. I want to ease into my morning and lie in bed for a good long time, half asleep, trying to think about what needs to be accomplished in my new day. How many of us feel similarly?

How many of us go through our lives half asleep and missing God's alarms, gifts, or opportunities? We prefer to live in a dream...lost in our thoughts about what we think should or will happen to us. We do this because it's easier. We think we have control—even though it's a false sense of control. The fact of the matter is, we have no control. We think we will accomplish goals by a certain age, live for a certain length of time, have 2.6 children, vacation here and there, etc., but, in reality, they are all self-created smokescreens that carry no guarantees at all. For example, last Tuesday, I was driving through the intersection of Route 202 and Glen Alpin Road in Harding Township, NJ, and was almost struck broadside and killed by a driver that completely ignored the red light. It all happened so fast, and I still don't know how he or she missed me. Was that driver lost in thoughts of what had to be done later in the day? All I know is that the rest of that day was much sweeter for me, knowing that it almost ended, and I hope the event also served as a wake-up call for the other driver.

God often gives us gifts, but I think we're too numb to realize many of them. Three days before Father's Day, 2008, my son Cory and I were fishing on a pond on Lloyd Road in Bernardsville, NJ. It's a good-sized pond filled with fish, enough to satisfy any young boy's fishing dreams and desires. I grew up just two hundred yards up the road from this very location, so I knew it well, having done my share of fishing and exploring at this spot when I was a boy.

The evening was warm and filled with memories for me. At dusk, Cory was taking his last few casts, and I was sitting on the wooden bridge that crosses the stream, lost in thought, remembering how my father took me down to the pond when I was eight years old to collect Spring Peepers, those half-inch-long frogs that sing so loudly but are so hard to spot. The pond at that time was drained for dredging, and as we walked through the mud, my father scooped up several of these frogs and put them in a jar. Tugging at his arms, wanting and eager to inspect our catch, I kept saying, "Show me the peepers, Daddy!"

Well, I must have been remembering very vividly because I actually heard myself exclaim, "Show me the peepers!" This exclamation stirred me out of my daydream, and it occurred to me that I had not seen Spring Peepers in person and up close since that time. I had tried to show them to Cory once. We had visited a swamp several years ago, armed with insect repellent and a collecting jar, intent on finding these tiny singers, but they managed to remain hidden under the grasses, and we came back not having found a single frog.

With the thought of my experience with my father and the image of these small frogs on my mind, I got up and walked up the gravel driveway to pack up my rod and our tackle box. As I bent down to get the tackle box, something moved quickly in the dim, grey light of the evening. Surprised and thinking it was a spider (I'm not a fan of spiders—especially the jumping kind), I recoiled, only to see about a dozen creatures hopping around the tackle box. Looking closer, I was amazed to realize that they were Spring Peepers! Imagine that! I picked one up and called Cory over to the spot to share the discovery with him. I let Cory hold the tiny creature in his hands and inspect it, and I recounted to him my similar childhood experience at that very same place.

When he was finished, we put the frog back where we found it, but the others were gone! None of the other frogs could be seen. The middle of a gravel driveway is not the environment or location to look for these creatures, but just a few minutes earlier, there they were, concentrated in one spot—the only spot where I would bend down to look. I couldn't get past the amazing thought that God gave me the peepers. Three days before Father's Day, forty years after I had seen them with my father, and minutes after asking to see them again, there they were, in plain sight, on a gravel driveway. And when I tried to find them again, they were gone, vanished as quickly as they had appeared. Driving home, I couldn't shake the feeling that something very special had just occurred. The event impacted me dramatically, and I am so very grateful for it. If I had been concentrating on other things—too numbed by other thoughts—and not been attentive and living in the moment, I would have completely missed this gift.

So, how many times does God try to get our attention but we just don't realize it? What are the roadblocks to these realizations, and how can we overcome them? I think the answers to these questions can be addressed in three steps.

First, ask yourself, "Who am I?"

I have an empty Odwalla smoothie bottle. The ingredients are listed on the label in descending order of volume: organic soymilk, organic oatmilk, banana purée, ground almonds, organic cane juice, vanilla extract, vitamin B6, and vitamin B12. If I were to list the ingredients based upon my senses, I wouldn't think that some of these ingredients were part of the recipe, nor would I know that some were organic. I just don't taste them. I don't sense them. I'm glad they're in there, but there's no way for me to tell just by tasting the product.

On an index card, make a list of your personal ingredients—things that make you who you are. For example, mine would list father, husband, writer, ministry programs director, songwriter, child of God, runner, etc. List six to ten of your ingredients. After you have done this, put them in order from most important (most volume) to less important (less volume). Now ask yourself these questions. How would others list your ingredients if they were making a label for you? Would they leave anything out? Would the priority order be changed? Then consider whether you would change your behavior in response to their list in order to more accurately reflect the real you? For example, writing is very important to me. If other people didn't realize that, it would inspire me to make my writing more prominent in my public life.

After you've thought about this for a while, consider this: What about God's list? What would God put on your ingredient list? What would God's order be, and would God's order inspire any kind of change in you?

You see, once you know your ingredients, you can better realize the events in your life that impact those ingredients, but, first, you have to recognize the events. There's a really wonderful activity called *Human Camera* that I've facilitated in teambuilding programs with corporate and student groups. It involves leading a person around with their eyes closed. Every so often, you position the person so they are pointed toward a particular item or scene, and you have them open their eyes for several seconds and "take a picture." After the shot is completed, the person closes his or her eyes and is led to the next shot, and so on. Eventually, the partners switch roles, and at the end of the activity, both partners sit down and explain what they "photographed" and why they chose their particular items as subjects. It's a fantastic way for people to experience how other people think and operate — to learn what's important to them as individuals. The activity also allows you to show others what is important for you to see in the world. I'm wondering…how would it be if we allowed God to show us what is important for us to see in the world? The photographs, I would guess, would be quite revealing.

Second, stay in the moment.

Think of this analogy to life. You're riding in a car, taking a tour of this place called Earth, and God is your tour guide and driver. Oh, you may choose different roads to take, but God knows where all the roads lead and knows your destinations. If you recognize that God is steering, this gives you the ability to sit back and survey the changing scenery outside your window, and this ability to survey gives you two things: freedom *and* responsibility. Certainly, you have the freedom to really "see" around you. You don't have to keep your eyes on the road to check traffic or look for road signs; you can look wherever you like, forwards or backwards, but looking out to the side provides the best view of the scenery you are passing at any given moment. Only passengers have this unique freedom because drivers are much too preoccupied with navigating and operating the car. However, this freedom also goes hand-in-hand with the responsibility to gather the experiences being presented to you. God is taking you places you have never been before, and each moment brings with it special gifts and visions and experiences that are meant just for you, many that are once-in-a-lifetime experiences!

This sounds pretty good, doesn't it? Well, if you believe that God puts you where you need to be, then open your mind to what you can draw or learn from each moment. People bring back as many photographs and memories as they can from their trips and vacations, so why not do the same with life? Many of us go around thinking of events that may occur later in the day, tomorrow, this week, next week, or beyond. We nod off while God is driving, lost in a waking dream or thinking of some future destination rather than paying attention to what God is showing us at that specific point in time. People do this at home, work, even church. The result is that this activity does not allow one to be fully present.

One of the things we know about ourselves is that the conscious, human mind can only focus on one thing at a time—one thing! Oh, we can go back and forth between two or more things very quickly, but at any given moment, we are only attentive to one thought. If I'm thinking about how pretty someone's dress is in the congregation, I'm not thinking about my sermon. If I'm thinking about where I need to be with my son this afternoon, I'm not concentrating on what is impacting me at the present time. Did you ever get lost in a thought while driving and "wake up" only to realize that there's a big gap in your driving route that you don't remember having driven at all? I do this from time to time, usually on a highway. They are reminders to me that I need to be more focused on the present, not only for safety, but for sheer appreciation of that which is going on around me.

We need to let events flow. There's a wonderful book by Jon Kabat-Zinn entitled *Wherever You Go, There You Are*. It's an amusing title, but it encapsulates the book's premise that we should pay more attention to where we are in our current lives rather than thinking about the future or the past. One of the analogies made by Kabat-Zinn equates experiencing life's events and our thoughts much like we would view a waterfall if we were in a cave behind the falls. We would see a continual cascade of water passing in front of our eyes, and we would be conscious of each portion of it for a moment, but then each water view would pass away and out of sight in order to make room for the next to come into view. The trick lies in the ability to let things go. Certainly, we need to concentrate on some things in life, but we also need to strike a balance between what we see and what we think. When we think too much, we miss the momentary gifts in our present awareness. As an experiment, I once changed my tie in the middle of a worship service. How many people would notice? Less than ten per cent of the congregation realized that I changed my tie. I began with a tie imprinted with American flags and finished wearing a blue tie with silver stars. For sure, changing a tie is not a big deal, but what if this was something more important, a more personal vision that God was presenting to you in your life?

We also need to let go of preconceived assumptions, and be prepared to be surprised. All of us assume far too much. I will live to be a certain age. I will have a specific type of home. I will attain certain milestones in my life. We have date books and digital calendars full of appointments and events that we assume we will attend, but there are no guarantees that *any* of them will happen. It's good to have an outline or reminders of things that we may plan, but leave room for the unexpected. Life's anger and aggravation and frustration are born out of events that run counter to our plans or perceived outcomes. This is a big one for me to manage and keep in mind, but you may find yourself in this group as well. God has a plan for my life—for all of our lives—and we need to prepare ourselves for God's surprises. Some will be joyous, and some will be difficult or sad. That's what life is like, but we need to remind ourselves that it all fits into God's plan. Our routes through life are going to be filled with difficulties and sheer exhilaration. The combination of the two and the unknown, mysterious quality of existence make life interesting and each experience a unique gift. Try to learn from each and every event life brings to you. Carry an umbrella and a basket of smiles, and prepare to be surprised by God.

Thirdly, look for connections among events.

If you know who you are and you stay in the moment, you will begin to realize that there are connections between and among the events of your life on a much more regular basis. This growing realization is quite extraordinary and rewarding. Of course, there is a price that must be paid for this. The payout involves making a continual effort to be more aware in your present life and to remember the people, things, and events that got you where you happen to be. Do you recall my story about the Spring Peepers? That event would not have been anywhere near as meaningful if I had not remembered my childhood excursion with my father.

In fact, I may not have even seen the Spring Peepers around my tackle box if I was scurrying to pack up and thinking more about leaving than I was about the present moment. Awareness takes effort, but it paves the way for abundant rewards. The payoff is that life will be richer, and you will be more fully aware of God's gifts and God's work in your life.

This relationship between God and man, between the Creator and the created, between awareness and realization is simply amazing. Work at it. Wake up to God's alarms, and let God show you the gifts and the riches prepared especially for you in your life.

Dog Daze

"A man's heart plans his way, but the Lord directs his steps."

~ Proverbs 16:9 ~

My dog, Aztec, has often reminded me much about people's relationship with God. I don't think it has anything to do with undiagnosed dyslexia and the fact that "dog" spelled in reverse is "god." It also isn't because I worship my dog, although I do seem to cater to his every need. No, I think it has more to do with the way Aztec behaves and responds to me.

One early July, I let Aztec outside to do what doggies do in the yard. A very long cable clipped to his harness allowed him to have access to most of the entire backyard. He was as happy as, well, a dog out there, so we tended to let him wander and dig and sniff and explore to his heart's content. Sometimes he just busied himself with reclining in the grass under the trees. As a result of this hedonistic, canine, Club-Med-type behavior, it wasn't uncommon for us to let him stay out for a good period of time. When he wanted to come back inside the house, he'd let us know by returning to and sitting at the back-door.

On this particular occasion, Aztec had been out for quite some time, and it had grown dark. When I went to look for him through the glass door, he was nowhere to be seen. Becoming concerned for Aztec, I went in search of him. Upon going outside to determine his whereabouts, I found him having completely tangled his lead around the legs of the trampoline. Aztec left himself with only two feet of cable for slack, but there he was, waiting patiently. He wasn't barking, he wasn't squirming, and he wasn't looking worried at all. If fact, he seemed to be in a daze, resigned to wait patiently for me. When he saw me, his relieved and happy expression seemed to say, "I knew you'd come to get me!" He was completely trusting, comfortable, and confident in the knowledge that I would find him, untangle him, and bring him back with me.

Later in the summer, during my family's trip to Maine, Aztec was again on a lead in the front yard of our vacation home. He was sniffing along the ground, intently following a scent trail of something particularly mesmerizing, and had completely lost track of his wanderings, oblivious to the web he was weaving with his lead around the legs of a picnic table. When he literally got to the end of his rope, he searched for a way out, and, not seeing one, simply looked up to me with an expression of "Uh-oh! Now what do I do?"

"Silly puppy," I said, "just follow your lead back to me."

In the moments that followed my saying that and guiding my dog in reverse through his self-constructed maze, I thought of it as an illustrative metaphor for some of our own interactions with God. Honestly, how often do we get tangled and find ourselves at a loss of knowing what to do? Lots of times, if you're like me. Do you say "Uh-oh?" Do you ask God, "What do I do?" Well, perhaps not in so many words, but when these situations occur, I imagine our Creator looking at us with compassion, the way I looked at Aztec underneath that picnic table, and saying, "Silly child, just follow the path back to me." If we don't see the way or can't figure it out for ourselves, God's word will direct us. We don't need to panic. We just need to trust God and wait for His response and guidance. It does no good to yell and scream, for these only add to the frustration.

When you get into a jam, when you're at the end of your rope and it looks as though you're hopelessly ensnared, look toward God. He will search out His lost children. If you really trust your Master, relax, explore your options. If you don't see a way out of your entanglement, look to God and ask, "Now what do I do?" Then, just wait and listen. Liberation and salvation are surely close at hand.

Raincoats

It was one of those summer weekends when the rain just wouldn't stop. The kind of rain that you can hear beating on the roof. The kind that makes you think—more than once—about water getting into your basement. All weekend it just poured.

My daughter must have been no older than five, and every trip we made out of the house was a study in staying dry. I'd get her wrapped up in her yellow raincoat to go to the food store and the mall. She would insist on getting the mail with me and walking our dog, and, of course, everywhere she went, she had to have her green boots and her pink umbrella with blue polka dots. The weekend was a flurry of raincoats, hats, hoods, umbrellas, and boots. We didn't have a garage, so the rain battered us as we ran to the car, buckled her into her car seat, sprinted between stores, and dashed back in the house. I spent an incredible amount of energy just trying to keep Melina and myself dry. Well, come Sunday afternoon, I had had enough of the wet weather. It was mid-afternoon, we were back from our last excursion out of the house, and I was done with the rain. I was completely rained out. Melina was bored, and I was cranky. We had been to the movies, and now running out of ideas of things to do indoors, I left Melina playing while I made popcorn.

Our weekend changed completely when Melina took it upon herself to let our dog out, and I heard one of the best sounds a parent can ever hear. My daughter was giggling so hard and she was excitedly calling Daddeee, Daddeee. Through the window, I saw that Melina had gone off the porch with the dog, no raincoat, and she was spinning around in the rain. She was calling for me to join her, and after a moment's hesitation, I did just that—and we had the BEST time! We played, we jumped, we splashed, we laughed…and we got absolutely soaked. It was the best thing we did all weekend. Melina liked it better than the movie, the trip to the mall, and any of the games we played inside because she was dancing with her father in the rain. I realized that it was MY perception of what was the correct thing to do in the rain that was causing my frustration. I was letting raincoats get in the way. Melina had the answer all along.

Sometimes we get so caught up in our own vision of how we think things "should be" or how we should act that we forget who's really in control. Our lives get spread so thin that we forget the treasure we have in God, and that means God gets spread too thin as well.

Did you ever hear this joke? A preacher and his flock at a very poor church in the hills of Tennessee took up collections, baked cakes, and washed cars for months to get enough money to buy paint for the church exterior which was bare and weather-beaten. Finally they went to Walmart and bought enough paint for the job, and all joined together on a Saturday morning to complete the job. When they were about half finished, they realized that they were going to run out of paint before finishing. The preacher said, "It's a water base paint, just thin it down with water." They continued painting and thinning until the color started losing its depth, and when they finally finished, the church was dark green at the top, light green in the middle and a very light green (almost white) at the bottom. The preacher and his flock were standing on a nearby hill admiring their work when a dark cloud appeared and the heavens opened up with a deluge of rain, which washed all of the newly applied paint off the church. The preacher was in tears, and the congregation was stunned at all the hard work they had done for nothing. Just then there was a huge lightning flash followed by the roll of thunder, and a loud voice from the heavens rang out, "REPAINT, REPAINT AND THIN NO MORE."

Now, if that were a real situation, I think God would have loved the paint job on that church—not in spite of its flaws, but because of its flaws. After all, the church isn't a building...it's the people in it. We are all unique individuals, and God has a plan for all of us, just the way we are. We don't have to pretend to be someone or something we're not. But sometimes we lose sight of this. We get sidetracked. We get so consumed with the raincoats in our lives that we don't let ourselves experience the Living Rain...the restorative Water of God.

What raincoats do we wear that keep us from washing ourselves in the love of God? What raincoats do we wear that prevent us from getting soaked in God's grace? I once had a youth service where all the worship leaders wore raincoats with different words applied to them. The words were things that often divert our attention from God or hamper our relationship with him. No one word was illustrative with any one individual because we're all human, and all of us, at some time or another, wear all of these raincoats. The trick is to try and shed these raincoats as often as possible and see how the spirit of God can change you. One at a time, as we shed our raincoats, we revealed different words, ones that could replace the original ones and bring us closer to God. Consider these, for example.

FEAR is a raincoat. We know we have sinned. It makes us feel bad, and we think that, perhaps, if we don't say anything, that God won't know. We are fearful of being judged by God. But if we come to God with all that junk, He can wash our sins, and our fear can turn to *TRUST*.

GREED is a raincoat. It's so easy to get caught up in the physical world and want more, more, more. We stockpile and spend so much time thinking about ourselves, that we lose sight of God. If we take off that raincoat, the greed gets washed away to reveal *CHARITY*.

APATHY is another raincoat. Sometimes we just don't care about God or God's world or God's people. But underneath apathy is God's gift of *DILIGENCE* and the ability to work for positive change.

Sometimes we wrap ourselves in ENVY. We look at what others have and desire it for ourselves, forgetting about the unique path that God has laid out for us. If we let God wash it away, it can be replaced with *ACCEPTANCE*.

PRIDE can keep us shielded from God. Many times we think we can do it all ourselves, and we don't want to ask God for help. But we need to ask for help. God wants us to ask for help. In place of pride, God will grant us *HUMILITY*.

Did you ever get angry at God? I know we all get angry with each other. ANGER is a big raincoat. It may even come complete with a matching umbrella and pair of boots. We think we know what our lives should be like, and when things don't go according to *our* plan, we get angry. We may even curse God or others. Let God in. Let Him wash away your anger and replace it with *FORGIVENESS*.

All of us go through periods of time when we DOUBT God or God's plan. We question whether God is there for us, especially during the trying times of our lives. Remind yourselves that your Creator is with you every step of the way, right beside you, and let the doubt transform into *CERTAINTY*.

RESENTMENT can be another barrier from God. We sometimes resent others for what they have, or we resent God for not giving us what we want. We treat God and others poorly, and, if not kept in check, it can snowball into hate. We need to ask God for help with this. Let God wash the resentment from your heart and, in its place, leave *KINDNESS*.

IDOLATRY is a raincoat. In our case, it may not be golden statues that we worship, but it may be money. It may be power. It may be a lifestyle. It may be a relationship. Take off your raincoat and be soaked in the *LOVE OF GOD*.

And now, I'd like to invite you all to think about what your raincoats might be. What is it that gets in between you and God? Imagine yourself removing that raincoat and feeling the deluge of God's love. Dance in God's grace. Lose yourself in His love as it rains down on you. Laugh hard, spin around, and excitedly call out to your Father in heaven. It will be the BEST thing you do.

Samaritan Cardinals

There is a place where I go to write. I sit on the back porch of an arboretum's eighteenth century, stone farmhouse in front of gardens and natural fields of grasses, wildflowers, birds, and other life. It is a serene and peaceful place, and it allows the words to flow out of me almost as if they are being channeled through an outside source.

One, warm, August day, I was desperately needing to jumpstart my writing—or at least my inspiration level—and this farmhouse seemed to be just what I needed. Settling into my porch chair, time dissolved away, as it so often does when creativity takes command. At times, I would gaze up and spy a number of Cardinals and Catbirds amongst the foliage of the surrounding trees, but the interlude didn't last long. In a matter of seconds, my eyes were back on my paper, and my mind was spinning with thoughts and words.

Suddenly, I heard a thump behind me. I recognized the sound from my childhood, and I knew immediately what had happened. Turning around in my chair, I saw something had fallen to the ground below the back door about fifteen feet from me. Wasting no time, I stood and hastened to the door and saw what I expected. There on the granite step below the door was a female Cardinal. She had become confused by the reflection in the door's glass and flown into it, thinking it to be open space. When I was a child, birds would often fly into the row of glass panes along the tops of my family's garage doors. Many times they would die instantly from the impact, but there were also several times when the birds would be dazed, and I would be able to nurse them back to health. On this occasion, the female Cardinal was lucky, for she lay slightly on her right side, eyes blinking, her beak opening and closing—almost as if she were trying to call for help.

Instinctually, I bent down and gently cradled the Cardinal in my hands and returned to the porch, trying to assess any injuries that the bird might have sustained. She appeared to be no worse for the wear. Her feet and legs supported her nicely in the palm of my left hand. She was looking around, aware of her surroundings, and holding herself upright. I even tested her wings by lifting my hand up and down, making her instinctually spread her wings as if beginning to fly. Her wings were not broken and worked splendidly. But this Cardinal just sat in my hand, very calmly, seemingly tamer than my son's pet parakeet. The stillness and total lack of fear in this wild bird's eyes was quite striking.

Just once did she make a move to fly, but it was really only a hop that she made off of my hand to the porch floor, a couple of feet below her. When I moved to pick her up again, she stepped willingly on to my hand. Obviously, the bird was stunned, so I took my time with her, walking around the grassy yard in front of the porch. It was then that I noticed a male Cardinal, chirping very nervously in a branch above our heads. "Could it be?" I thought. "Could this be this bird's mate?"

I decided to knock on the door of the larger house in hopes that someone there might offer to care for the bird. The house was a short trip up the driveway, which the two houses shared, so off I went. During the entire walk, the female Cardinal sat still in my hand, and keeping pace with us was her mate, flitting from branch to branch, remaining just ahead of us. Knocking on the door of the larger house did no good. Despite hearing music through an open window on the second floor of the house, it was apparent that either no one was home, or nobody could hear me.

My back-up idea was to try the barn, as I thought there might be a gardener there who could offer assistance. The stone barn was twenty yards or so further up the driveway, so on I went, accompanied by my stunned feathered friend and her nervous mate. I had learned once that Cardinals mate for life, and was impressed with the continuous concern this Cardinal had for his mate. If people were more like this, the world would be a better place, I thought.

As was the case with the house, I found there was no one at the barn either. After looking in a few windows, I looped around the side of the barn nearing the meadow. All at once, the female Cardinal hopped from my hand and flew about five yards under a shrub. Mirroring her flight was the male, but he alighted in a branch of a tree above her. This was a good sign! If she can fly, she'll be safe. Not entirely sold on the idea that she was fully recovered, I reached under the shrub and scooped the female into my hand.

There's a special feeling one gets when one is exposed to wildlife in such an intimate manner. I studied the fine feathers on her breast, felt the light scratch of her nails on my hand, and marveled at the depth inside her dark eyes. It was an experience I'll never forget, and it made me recall the biblical story of the

Good Samaritan. I really had no reason to take time from my day to save a bird, yet it was something I felt compelled to do.

I walked several more yards toward the meadow with the Cardinal in my hand. There was no mistaking the bond between the two birds in my midst. They had genuine concern for and awareness of one another, and I felt the lines between human and bird begin to blur. I like to think that I saved this bird, and their behavior had affected me as well. Was this a gift? Of course it was! What's more, I believe it was something I was meant to experience.

Just as I was considering this, I stepped from under the trees into the sunlight, and the female Cardinal took to flight. This time she appeared strong and stable, flying fifteen yards or so to a small tree on the opposite side of the meadow's fence, alighting on one of its lower branches. Like a shadow, the male followed her and landed on the same branch. Again, the story of the Good Samaritan entered my mind, but this time I wondered who had played the role of the Samaritan. Did I save the Cardinal, or did the Cardinals save me?

The Garden Well

"What makes the desert beautiful," said the little prince, "is that it hides a well somewhere…People where you live grow five thousand roses in one garden…yet they don't find what they're looking for…"

"They don't find it," I answered.

"And yet what they're looking for could be found in a single rose, or a little water…"

"Of course," I answered.

And the little prince added, "But eyes are blind. You have to look with the heart."

~ Antoine de Saint-Exupéry, "The Little Prince" ~

September is our second spring, filled with new beginnings. Our daily routines resume, refreshed from summer's leisure. School gets underway with new discoveries and challenges, and calendars get filled with our plans for the next nine months. It's exciting, but amidst all the hustle and bustle, we can often lose track of the simple gifts with which God continually surrounds us.

I spend a great deal of time writing in a garden that is part of Morristown National Historical Park. While I'm there, I notice people coming and going, walking from one flower bed to another, across fields and along trails, expending great amounts of energy and covering considerable amounts of space looking for peace or trying to harvest an array of diverse sights, thinking they have to go in search of life. Occasionally, I join them, but most of the time I just sit and observe.

Do you know what I've discovered? Life comes to you. Within a short amount of time, God can show me a well of wonder in that small garden: hummingbirds, rabbits, butterflies, chipmunks, people, planes, patterns in the clouds and brickwork paths, the warmth of the sun, floral fragrances that mix with the sound and whisper of a breeze, the kiss of light rain on my cheek, and the unique beauty in every single bloom. Most of these things are missed if we amble through the garden. We pass by so quickly that we startle and drive the creatures around us into hiding. A good deal of the environment becomes a blur, senses blending one into another without distinction. We can visit a place and often come away not really knowing it at all because we move too quickly. I think this is often the manner in which we interact with other people as well. It's not only our time spent that matters; it's our attention level within that time that makes the difference.

God gives us so much and lays a plethora of perceptions at our feet, but our senses become numb after a while. Our daily routines can draw a barren pall over our awareness. We need to open our hearts to see. We need to be willing to understand that God provides us with our needs and showers us with gifts right where we are. Sometimes they are enormous, and at times they are minute, but they are ever-present and close as our next breaths. And the secret? The secret is knowing we can learn and be enriched from every one of them, but we have to be able and willing to stop and observe.

At times, our world may seem like a desert, but God's well of promise lies just underneath the sands of our consciousness. In this garden of life, miracles can be found in a single blooming event. Seek them out and take note of them. Let the world come to you and spill out on your life. Let the ocean of God's well lap at your shores and wash you in abundance and grace.

The Meadow of Heaven

There is a difference between hearing and listening. I often find myself amazed at the way my brain screens and censors the sounds that fill my ears. Day-to-day existence is very much like going to the symphony and zeroing in on one instrument. I can get so focused on the solitary that I miss the plurality of the world around me. I'm trying to fix that.

One afternoon, I decided to visit a particular location in the Scherman-Hoffman wildlife sanctuary near my home, a place I had not visited in quite some time. I loaded my backpack, and off I went. As I walked the gravel road down past the sanctuary office, dozens of grasshoppers, startled by my presence, rose up like magical fairies from the stones and take wing, only to land and disappear once more into the road. I played a game with myself to see if I could see them before they sprang to flight, but, try as I might, I couldn't spot them against the stone and dirt. Time after time, they would surprise me, and time after time, as quickly as they had appeared, they would vanish into thin air upon landing, masterfully camouflaged by their shape and coloring.

My destination within the sanctuary ended up being a meadow, perhaps the size of a football field. It called me into it. The sun was bright and warm, and there was a slight breeze in the dry, early September air. It was one of those times that can make the mind wander back to those early autumn days of childhood when fathers and their children might fly kites. The setting had a timeless quality to it. As I reached the center of the meadow, I sat on a flat rock near the edge of the mowed, grass path and worked at being still. This may sound a bit silly to some, but the state of stillness really does involve a great deal of concentration and persistence. The biggest obstacle is daydreaming—an act into which it is easy to slip when one is quiet and surrounded by a lack of modern intrusions. For me, the key to being still is to let go of my thoughts and focus on my senses. It's not that I stop thinking; it's more that I don't hold on to the thoughts. I let them come and go like the clouds passing overhead. I'm aware of them, but I don't grab hold of them.

In the midst of my stillness, I was surprised by the sound of sighs. They started out hushed and barely perceptible, but then I realized it was the trees. They were watching me, surrounding the meadow in which I sat. Lines of them, masses of green and grey, round-faced, sun-dappled canopies and sharp-foliaged arms waved to each other and spoke a language that was familiar to my soul but remained unintelligible to my modern mind, which strained to understand. Carried by the wind, each tree in succession would begin to sigh and speak and bend toward its neighbor to share the secret. This continued until every tree was speaking a cacophony of messages, waving in a frenzy, shaking almost with jubilation at the message on the wind. Then all would go quiet, the arboreal telephone chain having run its course until another breeze carried in another message from the heavens, and then it would begin anew in a continual cycle of wooded gossip.

Just as I became aware and expectant of the sighing of the trees, my consciousness sharpened to a deeper level. I was surrounded by spirits. They stood all around me in every direction, long, green, and skeletal with heads gone to seed. They sprung up wherever I cast my eyes, tossing back and forth. The grass! The meadow was ablaze with little gods who now echoed the sighs of the trees with whispers that hissed and called and welcomed me into their midst. "Welcome, my son. Come and sit among us. You've been so long gone, and we've been waiting, waiting. Let us tell you of those who have come before us and have now returned to the soil beneath you." And the grass held out its green-bladed arms, drew me in, and sang a song of whispers until I became the grass in the meadow and the encircling trees. I was not just hearing; I was listening—listening and understanding that language of the soul—ancient, honest, direct, and whole.

I was not just looking; I was seeing—seeing a new world—but one to which I had always belonged. And then I saw them, here and there—angels—winged angels of every kind and shape and color that rose from the grass and flew in every direction of the compass. They were messengers upon which I had gazed before this day, but I didn't understand. I wasn't able to really see. My mind always got in the way, and I couldn't see past their names and taxonomy, their earthly labels with which I categorized everything in sight. To me, they were American Goldfinches, the Widow Skimmer dragonfly, and the Little Wood Satyr, Banded Hairstreak, and American Copper butterflies, but now I saw them for what they were beneath their earthly cloaks. They were holy messengers sent to share with me the secret. It was, ironically, the most basic of truths—that we are no different from the trees or the grass or other life forms that inhabit the world. Oh, we may take different physical forms, but the life force that binds us all is one and the same.

During all of this, shadows had begun to creep across the meadow, and from behind me a chorus of crickets was singing with rhythmic chirps. They, too, sang the same message. And all the while, it filtered and blended and seeped into my mind. The lyrics of the crickets' song, the whisper of the grass, the sighing of the trees, and the messages of angels whirled into a cyclone of awareness. Then the visitation occurred—a red and black angel appeared right beside me. This glorious Red Admiral butterfly alighted on my backpack, inches from my elbow, and it rested and slowly unfolded and closed its wings three times—that holy number whose significance was not unnoticed by me. I was changed. I was ready. I was fulfilled and bursting with the joy of this awareness, this truth granted by working at stillness in a meadow.

With an alacrity that equaled its arrival, the red and black angel took flight, ascending upward and across the field. I lost it in the boughs of trees, but it seemed to be transfigured, for at the very moment I lost sight of the Red Admiral, a Red-tailed hawk took flight from the canopy and flapped overhead until it began to glide in ever higher circles above my head. It was as if it were leading me out, leading me away, blazing a trail, and beckoning me to follow. And so I arose and walked the narrow path out of the meadow, away from the field of gods and angels, away from myself and within myself, following the one in flight that led the way to see and listen to our one essence. The world was in the meadow, yet the meadow was in the world, and both exist within the realm of heaven.

Indian Summer

From his pipe the smoke ascending
Filled the sky with haze and vapor,
Filled the air with dreamy softness,
Gave a twinkle to the water,
Touched the rugged hills with smoothness,
Brought the tender Indian Summer
To the melancholy north-land,
In the dreary Moon of Snow-shoes.

~ Henry Wadsworth Longfellow ~

The term, Indian summer, dates back more than two hundred years. The earliest known use was by the French-American writer, St. John de Crevecoeur, who lived in rural New York in 1778. The etymology of Indian summer indicates that the time period relates to when the First Nations/Native American peoples would harvest their fall crops. It's a beautiful time of the year splashed with the warm colors of the leaves and carrying the reminder that we need to pull out our woolen sweaters, hats, and gloves. Despite the cooling temperatures, I've always found Indian summer to be a heart-warming time of year.

I've been wondering—can one have a spiritual Indian summer? I believe it's something that happens to all of us. Think back on the times in our lives when people and opportunities seem to be ebbing away, or the wake of some large event leaves us feeling a bit empty. Children go away to school, vacation has ended, we feel stuck in a rut at work, home, or in a marriage. Things are not necessarily bad, but the vibrancy is waning. We've all been there; it's part of life.

Then, in the midst of the growing chill, something miraculous and unexpected occurs. It may come in the form of a warm comment from a friend or loved one. Perhaps it's a piece of blissful news that arrives via the phone, E-mail, or letter. Whatever it might be, an agent of change arrives on the wind to shift our mindset, and our lives take on a renewed life and energetic pulse, and we feel recharged as a direct result of this event.

Every one of us has the capacity to be the agent of positive change. God can work through all of us to bring a spiritual Indian summer to those around us, and, in doing so, we often find a renewed connection to God. When I was a child, I had this Matchbox car and track, and one of the track pieces had a motorized set of opposing, spinning, rubber wheels that would propel the car with just enough force to send it around the loop again. Once set in motion, the car never stopped.

Wouldn't it be great if we did that for each other? Wouldn't it be wonderful to display our faiths through simple acts that brought warmth and vigor back into other's lives? We all do it, but perhaps, at this time of year, when the chill is building in the air, we can be more conscious of how we can warm each other's hearts. We can help people harvest joy. We can be the winds of change that bring about a spiritual Indian summer, no matter what season it happens to be. Perhaps we could even write our own version of Longfellow's poem.

> *From our souls the warmth unending*
> *Filled the earth with joy and vigor,*
> *Filled the air with faith-filled harvest,*
> *Bring a twinkle to our brothers,*
> *Touch the rugged hearts with kindness,*
> *Bring a sacred Indian Summer*
> *To our melancholy neighbors.*
> *Share the joy of God with others.*

True Nature

What color are you? Deep under your skin—in your heart and soul—what is your true nature?

I once stood outside of my home on a perfect, mid-September morning. Brilliant sunshine warmed the air, which held not even the slightest hint of humidity, and a gentle breeze rustled in the leafy branches of the trees above my head. The sound drew my attention skyward, and as I gazed into the top of a nearby Sweetgum tree, I noticed a small, vivid patch of yellow amidst a sea of emerald foliage and cerulean sky. One small section of the tree's leaves, perhaps a dozen or so, had turned color for the fall, and it was beautiful.

Do you know why deciduous leaves change color in the autumn? There are three types of pigment involved in autumn leaf colors. Chlorophyll gives leaves their basic green color. Trees use chlorophyll for photosynthesis, the chemical reaction that enables plants to use sunlight to manufacture sugars for their food. Carotenoids produce yellow, orange, and brown colors in leaves and other things such as corn, carrots, daffodils, and bananas. Finally, there are anthocyanins, which, in addition to leaves, also give color to such familiar fruits as cranberries, red apples, concord grapes, blueberries, cherries, strawberries, and plums.

Both chlorophyll and carotenoids are present in the chloroplasts of leaf cells throughout the growing season, but most anthocyanins are produced in the autumn, in response to bright light and excess plant sugars within leaf cells. During the growing season, chlorophyll is continually being produced and broken down and leaves appear green. However, as the length of night increases in the autumn, chlorophyll production slows down and then stops, and eventually all the chlorophyll is destroyed. At this magnificent, magical point, the carotenoids and anthocyanins that are present in the leaves are unmasked and show their colors.

Similar to the chlorophyll in leaves, we all wear masks that hide our true selves. We manufacture facades that we present to the world for protection, image, self-confidence, and to make certain impressions. We see it in the clothes we wear, the material goods with which we surround ourselves, and many other trappings of our way of life. For those of us who step out of the norm from time to time, it doesn't take long before we are noticed for our unusual nature, much like the yellow leaves I saw at the top of the Sweetgum. If we're fortunate, we're viewed as beautiful, but most of the time, we're just labeled as different.

This leads me back to my initial question. Deep under your skin, in your heart and soul, what is your true nature? Sometimes we get glimpses of it during the dark times of our lives. Like the tree leaves, as the length of our "nights" increase, as the troubled times of our existences surround us, we don't pay as much attention to our facades that we use to make our way through the world, and we open up ourselves to God. Our true colors are revealed in unabashed displays of magnificent imperfections, and it is at this time—when we are stripped down to our basic essence—that we become most unique, most human, and most open to God's grace and love. This love of God's is always there. All too often, we don't let it radiate from our hearts or let it penetrate our facades, yet it is during this state of being emotionally stripped that we are most glorious. There is us, and there is God, and nothing obscures the view.

Let us learn from the autumn leaves. Year after year, they only manage to show their colors for a brief period of time—just once—before they drop to the ground. They have to do this for the sake of their tree's survival. We however, are attached to a much different life source, the Living Vine, one that wants to shine through us every day of our lives.

Be daring! Don't simply read this and put it out of your mind. Look closely. Try to reveal and see the true nature of yourself and others at work in a world rooted in God. Take a good, hard look within and around you. Old things are passed away; behold, new things have come. Isn't life beautiful?

Einstein's Oversight

Say something to us we can learn
By heart and when alone repeat.
Say something! And it says "I burn."

~ Robert Frost, "Choose Something Like a Star" ~

The autumn's evening air was brisk, so much so that I needed my winter coat to keep me warm on my walk through the restricted management area of the Great Swamp National Wildlife Refuge. I was on a Sunset Walk with a group of perhaps eight or nine other individuals, drawn by the common goal of witnessing the myriad of ducks that congregate in the refuge at dusk. It's hard to understand how thousands of ducks and geese can be so close to New Vernon and go relatively unnoticed by most of us as we move through our daily routines, but we were promised they were there. Sure enough, as we stood still, flock after flock came in from their feeding grounds and the gathering October darkness to the sanctuary of the swamp. An expert could identify them by call and flight pattern…woodies, mallards, teal, blacks, widgeons, and pintails. I was witness to and immersed in a wild and ancient event. The waterfowl congregated in flocks that communicated to each other in hushed tones in the waning light. We all heard the birds, but I thought I also heard God whisper in the breeze, "I burn."

…and the more awesome God becomes.

During the walk back from the migration observation, we were stopped along the trail to listen to the silence. Actually, we were listening to something within the silence. The winged predators of the night were reestablishing their mating bonds. Low and muffled, it echoed out of the trees…"hooo-h'HOO-hooo-hooo."

The lonesome call of a Great Horned Owl pierced the darkness, followed shortly afterwards by the tremulous wail of a little Eastern Screech Owl somewhere far off in the woods. To someone who knows nothing of the night and the animals that dominate the darkness, these sounds may be frightening, but we found them calming and exciting. Owls, due to their feather structure, are absolutely silent on the wing, so they are most often located by their calls alone, except for the occasional silhouette that may pass overhead in a moonlit sky. Our leader imitated the little owl's wail, and we were amazed when it called back to us. We all heard the call, but I wondered if it might also be God that said, "I burn."

…and the more awesome God becomes.

Eventually, we returned to the parking lot, but just before we got into our cars, the leader focused his high-powered spotting scope on the clear, night sky. There was a bright planet rising in the southeast. Was it Venus? Mars? Perhaps Saturn? It turned out to be Jupiter, the giant planet that is approximately 450 million miles away from the Earth. This number seems large to us, but it is a mere speck when compared to the vast expanse of the universe. We all took turns looking through the scope and across the heavens to view not only Jupiter but four of its sixty-three moons as well! We all saw them clearly, but I think I saw something else…it was God's footprint in the sky that reminded me of the words I heard earlier, "I burn. I exist. And of all the wonders in nature and the universe, I choose to hold you in the palm of my hand."

Albert Einstein once said, "The more I learn, the more I realize how much I don't know." I feel he committed an oversight, for we would do well to continue his statement by adding *…and the more awesome God becomes.*

The Instinctual Life

Something tells the geese when it's time to fly south in the autumn. I'm not going to get bogged down in the biological causes and stimuli. Suffice it to say that it's something unseen, something instinctual, and something almost magical that makes these birds pick up and leave for warmer climates. I marvel at the enormous flocks of geese I witness every year cutting across the sky. At times they are so high that it's their calling that first stirs my curiosity and beckons my attention, and it's only after straining to scan the sky at high altitudes that the faint, dark V-shape of their flock is seen. Often, I am in awe of their ability to trust their instincts and follow where the rhythms of life lead them. I wish I could do this half as well as the geese. On occasion, I've had the fortune to spot a Snow Goose on the wing, among the more common Canada Geese, and have wished I could glimpse one on the ground.

One mid-October, I was driving to a lecture I was giving in an area of New Jersey that was unfamiliar to me. I arrived early, so as to avoid the rush hour traffic on Interstate 287. I asked a local about where I might get dinner and got directions to a location just a couple of miles from where I was to speak that evening. Perfect! I had just enough time to eat before setting up my equipment, as long as I moved quickly.

Well, by now there were a good number of commuters jamming the roads, but the directions seemed simple enough to follow: down the road three miles, turn right at the light, and go several miles to a mall. Due to the trees, the mall came into sight rather suddenly at a traffic light, so I turned right, reacting almost instinctually at the last second, expecting to find a way to enter the parking lot from the side road. Instead, I soon discovered with a good deal of frustration, that there was no left turn allowed from the side road. I was forced to continue up the road, crowded with cars, all the while looking for a place to turn and reverse my direction. There wasn't any such place for well over a mile.

Finally, with frustration building and an eye on the clock, I spied a field on the left that was under development, and it had a dirt road leading into it that was used by construction vehicles. This was my opportunity, so I took advantage of it. Having a break in the oncoming flow of traffic, I turned left onto the dirt road and swung my car around to face the road. Of course, now I had to wait for another break in traffic, so I could pull out on the road again. Biding my time, with anxiety mounting, I gazed out over the field. Something caught my eye. There in the middle of the field was a flock of Canada Geese, and among the multitude of birds was a spot of white, a Snow Goose! It looked so very majestic with its black wing tips set off against the pure-white plumage. I had wanted to see one for years, and there it finally was, directly in front of me.

Suddenly, the traffic and the clock and my dinner didn't matter. I was looking at a Snow Goose, and it occurred to me that I would not have seen it had I not been pulled in that direction by my miscalculation. Or…was it a miscalculation? Perhaps, I thought, perhaps I was meant to find that road that had no entrance to the mall. Perhaps this sighting was a gift that was planned for me. When I turned suddenly onto that side road beside the mall, I reacted without consideration, without contemplation. I turned out of instinct. However, when my expectations weren't met, I lost faith in the direction I was headed.

Why? Why don't we trust our instincts more often? Why don't we trust where life leads us? I had considered this question before, but the experience with the Snow Goose sighting made me revisit it more seriously. The Snow Goose doesn't question where it's drawn any more than autumn leaves question where the flow of a river will take them. Instincts guide the geese, river water carries the leaves, and God leads us all to places we're supposed to be. Too often, we fight our "mistakes," we get angry and frustrated at events that don't meet our expectations when, in reality, they are actually surprises from our creator.

Too much of our lives is centered on control, so I've decided to make a change. There is much we can learn from life, and I'm going to make an effort to step back and enjoy the surprises that life and God have in store for me. Maybe you'll want to try this with me. What will it be like to deny frustration, to allow ourselves to do more floating down life's river? I imagine it will feel like flying, like the flight of a Snow Goose sailing through the crisp, autumn sky.

What's in a Name?

"God once spoke to people by name.
The sun once imparted its flame.
One impulse persists as our breath;
The other persists as our faith."

~ Robert Frost, "Sitting by a Bush in Broad Sunlight" ~

The groan of the garbage truck roused me from my bed just in time to witness the first light of day painting the tops of the trees outside my window. Like most mornings, the initial order of business is to walk my dog, Aztec, so I hurriedly slipped the leash around his neck, a jacket on my back, and both of us out the door.

While the driver remained in the cab, the other garbage man was heaving bags of trash over the fence and into the back of the truck. I walked Aztec around the back of the house, eventually appearing from around the other side. I made eye contact and exchanged a cursory wave with the garbage man, who had since climbed into the passenger seat of the cab. The truck was now parked in the lot beside the church with its engine off. After continuing to stroll for a bit, I found myself passing through the lot. Deciding to say hello to this man who hauled away our trash twice a week, I approached the garbage man and said, "Good morning." What proceeded was totally unexpected.

"You don't mind us parked here, do you?" the garbage man asked.

"Doesn't bother me one bit," I answered.

"We're waiting until it's our time to go up to the lake. Is that a pit bull?" inquired the garbage man.

"No. It's an Australian Shepherd," I replied.

"From a distance, the brindle markings on the coat reminded me of a pit bull."

"You must love the extra light you get in the mornings with the time change," I said, changing the subject.

"It's not bad, but we start at two o'clock in the morning. Any way you cut it, it's dark when we go to work."

We continued chatting about this and that... trivial conversation, really... until we hit on Halloween. I had mentioned that I was just at the lake, trick-or-treating a couple nights earlier with my son, Cory. It had been a rainy night, and I described how the rain had begun to fall hard when we were furthest from our car. The walk back, almost the length of the lake, probably earned Cory extra candy due to the pity factor, as I'm sure we appeared quite drenched when we stopped at the houses.

The garbage man told me that he had gone out for Halloween as well. He had taken his two-year-old son, dressed as a pirate, around his neighborhood, and they were both having a lot of fun. Going door-to-door, I heard how it started to rain on them as well. His son, unfazed, still wanted to go to more houses, so they didn't let the rain stop them. Instead, the garbage man took off his rain jacket, wrapped it around his son, picked him up in his arms, kept him warm and dry, and carried him for the rest of the evening. The garbage man got soaked, but his son had fun and smiled the whole way home.

After hearing his touching story, I said I had to get my son ready for school, so I extended my arm up to the window of the garbage man's truck to shake his hand.

"My name's Gordon."

The garbage man lowered his hand to reach mine, but stopped just before making contact. He looked me in the eyes for a long second, a pause that seemed unusual to me, before he spoke.

"Thank you," he said. "My name's Rich."

He thanked me for speaking to him, for shaking his hand. That moment stayed in my mind for the remainder of the day. There are people out there who, due to careers or positions in life, are ignored or passed over. It may seem like they operate on the fringes of our lives, but they are immersed in this world as much as anyone else. Sometimes we know things intellectually, but they don't hit home until we experience them at a visceral level. Rich is no different than you or me. He goes to work to pay his bills and sustain his family, but the most joy he gets from his life comes from being a parent and caring for the people he loves. I had no preconceived goal in mind and no idea what the conversation I had with him would yield, but I can tell you this. As much of an impact that this conversation and handshake had on him, his reaction had a greater impact on me.

We are all connected in God's plan. We all have common ground and walk similar paths. Getting personal makes this more apparent. What's in a name? Sometimes everything. Thank you, Rich.

Harvest Home

"My long two-pointed ladder's sticking through a tree
Toward heaven still,
And there's a barrel that I didn't fill
Beside it, and there may be two or three
Apples I didn't pick upon some bough.
But I am done with apple-picking now.
Essence of winter sleep is on the night,
The scent of apples: I am drowsing off..."

~ Robert Frost, "After Apple-Picking" ~

I don't know about you, but there is something about Robert Frost's poetry that speaks to my heart very clearly. It might be his simple choice of words, his phrasing, or his iambic pentameter. Perhaps it's all of these traits or something less tangible that always invites a sense of familiarity and comfort when I read his works.

I don't know quite why, but there seem to be religious and spiritual metaphors that jump out at me when I read. One example in the above excerpt from "After Apple-Picking" is the ladder pointing toward heaven. It conjures up images of Jacob's ladder. The apple itself harkens back to the story of Adam and Eve and the traditional, much-maligned apple out of which they took those fateful bites.

I don't know if it was during my first reading of this poem or my second or my thirtieth, but I began to see other metaphors in the poem as well—hidden ones that are not as blatant as Jacob's Ladder and the Garden of Eden. When I read the entire poem, I begin to see the ladder as the harvester's life. It begins at the ground and proceeds, rung by rung, toward heaven. At the beginning, there is not much to pick, for our fruits appear only after we have worked and climbed to a certain level in our lives. Life's accomplishments become our apples. In time, our labors result in crops that ripen and can be harvested. Some crops are lean, and others are plentiful, and we make plans to pick. We reach and stretch, harvesting as many apples as possible, mindful that, as the traditional hymn states, "All is safely gathered in, ere the winter storms begin."

I don't know if it's due to my method, but not all of my apples end up being successfully picked. Some fruits make it safely into the basket. Others fall to the ground, bruised and cut, but even these can be used for cider or food for farm animals and wildlife. All of our actions lead to a product. We know the harvest will come to an end. We rush to beat the frosts of winter, and we tire. Life takes a great deal of energy. We long for rest, and eventually we hope to slip into that eternal sleep immersed in the heady scent of our harvest—our family, our loves, and our accomplishments—all safely stored away for spring, for the following generation, and we drowse off into the arms of God.

So, we are faced with a few important questions. What type of fruit are we harvesting in our lives? Hopefully our actions will yield the type of crop that is pleasing to both us and God. In addition to this, how much fruit will our crop yield? If we walk in kindness and spread goodness throughout our lives, the bounty will be considerable. Lastly, what happens to the fruits that we cannot reach, that go unpicked or fall to the ground despite our best efforts?

I don't know about you, but I feel secure in the knowledge that whatever apples I drop or fail pick in my life, well, they will be harvested by God.

The Child as Pilgrim

Harvest season is a time of icons. Thanksgiving brings us images of Pilgrim men in black breeches, square white collar and cuffs, wide buckled belts, and black steeple hats with a buckle. We also see Pilgrim women wearing full, black skirts, white aprons, and dark capes. Then there are the illustrations of face-painted, feather-adorned Native Americans carrying corn, pumpkins, and those colorful, fat, tom turkeys. Still, the best turkey icons are the ones children make by tracing their hand so that their thumb becomes the neck and head of the bird while their fingers become the fan of the tail. Churches resonate with the singing of "We Gather Together," and schools help our children remember how the Native Americans helped the Pilgrims by giving them food and offering them guidance and advice, despite their different appearance and customs. These signs of the holiday have been stamped into our memories since childhood.

We like to think of Pilgrims as belonging to another time, but children bear striking resemblances to them. Did you ever look up the word *pilgrim*? It is defined as "a person who journeys, especially a long distance, to some sacred place as an act of religious devotion," or as "a traveler or wanderer, especially in a foreign place." Children are pilgrims. Childhood is a pilgrimage. As adults, continuing on our own journey, we might do well to think of ourselves as playing the part of the Native Americans, the ones with experience who guide and advise those who have just arrived on this path with us.

As children of God, we are all moving toward a sacred place, and the entire span of our lives can be viewed as an act of religious devotion. It would be easy to ignore our new arrivals or think of them as strange because of their manner of dress, hairstyles, or choice of music, but essentially, we are all riding the same ship, the same *Mayflower* to a promised land. In this time of Thanksgiving, let us all celebrate the ties that bind us together. We might ponder the words that psychiatrist Robert Coles wrote in his book *The Spiritual Life of Children*.

> So it is we connect with one another, move in and across space and time—all of us wanderers, explorers, adventurers, stragglers and ramblers, sometimes tramps or vagabonds, even fugitives, but now and then pilgrims: as children, as parents, as old ones about to take that final step, to enter that territory whose character none of us here ever knows. Yet how young we are when we start wondering about it all, the nature of the journey and of the final destination.

A Gift Outright

I didn't remember anything about what he told me as I tried to brush the sleep from my eyes and staggered half-awake into the bathroom on a particularly cold Friday morning in December. Stumbling down the darkened hallway, I called, as I do almost every morning, for Cory to wake up—a hard thing for a boy of ten years old to do—and closed the bathroom door. Having felt the sensation of the soft, insulated carpet change to the hard coldness of the bathroom floor, I fumbled for the light switch, squinting to shield my eyes from the sudden, harsh, white light. Taking a moment to adjust, I pulled back the curtain, turned on the shower, waited for the water to get hot, and stepped into the steaming jets. The rest is a blur of suds and steam until I found myself reaching for my towel, and there it was, on the mirror — one of the most wonderful gifts I've received in a long, long time.

The night before had been filled with activity, and Cory was taking longer than normal to get ready for bed. Yelling up the stairs, I asked what was taking so long. "I'm making you a present," was his reply. "I'll call you when I'm finished. I promise." Well, by the time he called me, I had forgotten about what my son had said he was doing, so, when I got up to his room to say good-night, the thought of a present wasn't even on my radar. I tucked him in, kissed him on the head, closed his door, and headed down the stairs. A few hours later found me climbing into my own bed where sleep came quickly.

By the time morning came, I was only thinking about what it was that I needed to do that day. I was entrenched in my plans and schedule until they were all instantly washed from my mind by the gift that was displayed before me as I stepped out of the shower. My mirror had a rainbow on it. It wasn't a colored rainbow, it was a simple drawing, but to me it was a masterpiece — lines formed by my son who had drawn on the fogged mirror with his finger after his shower the previous night. I hadn't seen it on Thursday night or Friday morning because steam was needed to reveal the drawing, but my son knew I would see it after my shower. In front of me was a three-foot-wide rainbow with the names of colors printed in the arches. Above and beside the rainbow were the words, "Yellow and blue are my favorite colors," which they are. And below the rainbow, printed in big letters were the words, "I love you."

Okay, as a father I was blown away by this gift, a gift that I didn't even see—a gift that I had been promised but had forgotten. What's more, I felt a little guilty because I remember I had been feeling frustrated with Cory's bedtime progress on Thursday night. I assumed he was dawdling and wasting time, while, in reality, he was thinking of me…preparing a gift for me to be discovered at a predetermined time. Well, as you might have already guessed, I thanked my son immediately, giving him a big hug and telling him how surprised I was. What's more, he was thrilled that I noticed his present, sporting a huge grin on his face because he had made me happy.

Later in the day, this event kept spinning in my mind, and it reminded me of how God takes care of us. He prepares a table for us. He fills our lives with gifts, many of which we don't see or notice. Many times it's not until our lives get clouded—much like that bathroom mirror—that we truly see and experience how much He thinks of us, cares for us, and provides for us. Sometimes, on challenging days, my humanity gets the better of me, and I catch myself wondering if God's forgotten about my concerns—much like I wondered if my son was paying attention. But if I look closely, I see signs that He never loses sight of us. God surrounds us with gifts and reveals them to us according to His plan. And we should give thanks—often—for a gift outright deserves acknowledgement. I would like to think that God smiles when we tell Him His gifts make us happy. Look around you. Look every day but especially when it's hard to see, when you find yourself stumbling, when your life is cloudy. There, where you might not have seen it before, are His rainbows, filled with your favorite colors, and written in His hand are His words, His promise… "I love you."

In Eclipse

It could be that our faithlessness is a cowering cowardice born of our very smallness, a massive failure of imagination. If we were to judge nature by common sense or likelihood, we wouldn't believe the world existed.

~ Annie Dillard ~

Our ruddy satellite stared back at me, almost as if it were embarrassed, flushed in its fleeting mask. Standing in the cold and veiled by the darkness of the wee, morning hours of the winter's solstice, the total eclipse of the moon left me breathless and moved me to fascination.

Very early on December 21st, 2010, many people around the world were able to witness a phenomenal and rare, total lunar eclipse, watching as the Earth passed directly between the sun and the full moon, shrouding it in shadow and transforming the moon's white visage into a stunning, deep red glow. The event was especially significant, as it coincided with the winter solstice, something that hasn't occurred since 1638, when it was the first astrological event recorded in America, and won't come around again until 2094.

The reason why the moon turned red during the eclipse is, in itself, a beautiful concept. Recall, if you will, the most scarlet sunrise and fiery sunset you can remember. Now, imagine yourself on the moon during a total eclipse. You would look back at the Earth, which would appear much larger than the sun from your perspective, and witness our planet creeping across the face of the sun until the Earth entirely blocked the sun's direct light. When the sun was completely covered, one would see a ring of luminous, red light appear around the Earth's perimeter—the red light of every sunset and every sunrise going on at Earth at that moment—and it would last for a full seventy-two minutes! How awesome it would be to bask in that light, to witness the points where sunrise meets sunset! It's no wonder the ancients were awestruck with fear and wonder during celestial events, and it's no wonder I found myself wrapped in coat and blankets on my front lawn bearing witness to this solstice spectacle.

I could have filled my mind with thoughts of planetary orbits, gravitational forces, and the breakneck speed of billions of whirling, celestial bodies hurtling through the heavens, but my thoughts went to something more elemental, something outside the mathematics of astronomy and the common sense of modern man. I thought of God and His creations. Much like the relationship between our moon and sun, I thought of how we all reflect the perfect light of God, the blindingly beautiful light of creation, with all that we are.

Most often, we take the Light of the World for granted, although all of us ascend to consciousness and revelation at some point. We rise like divers breaking the surface of the pool of existence and fill our lungs with life, but there are also times when we miss God's light, when we dive too deep to see the surface. We overlook it most when we fancy we are shielded from it, when troubles crowd our small minds and limited imaginations, when things get in our way — things that appear to be larger than God, when we forget that God is eternal and constantly loving us and caring for us. But it's during those times of darkness, our times of personal eclipse, that God sees us in a different light. He knows our suffering and our pain on an intimate level because He was once a man, because He endured human pain, because He has experienced loss and sacrifice. What's more, He knows that His light will outshine our personal solstices, that the darkness in our minds will not last forever. He sees all of our sunsets, but He also knows of all of our sunrises, so He realizes when our dark times will end. He can see the points where our sunsets meet our sunrises, all of them, all at once, from birth to rebirth. What a spectacular vision that must be! What an astonishing God we have — well beyond comprehension through science, common sense, or likelihood!

Suddenly, a song by Chis August began playing in my head.

"I'm giving my life to the only One who makes the moon
reflect the sun.
Every starry night, that was His design.
I'm giving my life to the only Son, who was and is and yet to come.
Let the praises ring, 'cause He is everything."

These lives we spin out on this planet are beautiful. The light and shadow, the different moods and phases of our years, they are all transitory. Our times of light and dark are part of our Creator's plan, and they all point to a time when we will no longer be in eclipse, a promise of a time when we will all escape these earthly shadows and reflect and rest in the light of the Son forever.

Things We Get to Do

I don't know what it was…the pre-holiday energy shift, the routine of daily life kicking into gear, or the myriad of other things that impact one's day…but I found myself declaring on a December afternoon, "If there's one more thing that I *HAVE* to do, I'm gonna lose it!"

I guess we've all been there, and we've all been on the receiving end of an unexpected, and perhaps undeserved, abrupt rebuttal from someone under pressure. We duck for cover after asking what we thought was the most minor question or favor. What is it about stress that seems to lead us down that road to psychotic rants? What is it that turns us into schizophrenic Jekyll and Hydes? Can you relate to the situation of being a mild mannered professional by day only to transform into an impatient, Type-A lunatic as soon as you hit traffic on the highway? Ah-ha! If we could figure that one out, we could retire on book royalties alone!

So…what do you have to do today? What do you have to do this week, this month, next month? No doubt, our answers can feel burdensome and overwhelming. However, occasionally it's in the midst of frenetic abstraction that we can find glimpses of resolution.

In my case, it was on one of those days when everything exploded at once. I was sure the universe was out to get me — just me, mind you! Yes, the stress gods had surely awoken in a bad mood, reached into their bag labeled "Humans to Annoy," and pulled out my name. It's safe to say that they wasted no time putting their devilish plans into action.

My son got up late and was moving like molasses on an ice cube. We both hurried to shower before the hot water ran out. There was a huge, lethargic traffic snag on my way into work. I arrived at the high school where I was teaching to find a slew of E-mails I had to answer, five classes to teach, one class to cover, two tests to administer and correct, a stack of papers for each of my classes that needed to be read and graded, seven college recommendation letters to write, and a mandatory department meeting during lunch. On top of these, there was a looming deadline from my publisher I had to meet, and there were several Christmas shopping trips I had to fit in somewhere. The hectic pace was only accentuated by the thought that I had to pick up my son at his school, somehow get to the food store, immerse myself in my role as homework enforcer, and cook dinner...all by 6:00 PM. I also knew that after dinner and dealing with my son's bedtime, there would be bills to pay, clothes to wash, and classes to plan. Later that afternoon, becoming only slightly successful in emerging from my cloud of frenzy, I saw that it was already 3:15, that special time to brave the roads and the elongated, sluggish car line at my son's school. Well, while I was in my car, I switched on the radio, and, of course, my music station had a news break, which, of course, was filled with tragedy, fears, poverty, suffering, and bad news. Oh, the joy I felt! (Note the sarcasm.) What do I *have* to endure next?!...

I don't know why, but somehow out of the blue I was suddenly struck with a new perspective on things, and all I had to do was change one little word...*one little word*. The revelation was illuminating and liberating. Can I share a secret with you? You see, all of those things I think I *have* to do, are really things I *GET* to do. I *get* to wake up in the morning, shower in hot water, and choose clothes to wear. I *get* to rouse my son from slumber and bring him to school. I *get* to work in a career I love with extraordinary people. I *get* to express myself through writing and meet deadlines, shop for gifts, and even attend a meeting every now and then. I *get* to pick up my son from a great school. I *get* to buy groceries, prepare dinner, and sit with my son while he learns in our own warm home. I *get* to tuck him into bed, throw a load of laundry into a washer and dryer, and plan my meetings. Dare I say it? I even *get* to pay bills! My God, I thought, how You have blessed me! How many people would give anything to have only one of these blessings!

Every breath is actually a gift from God. Many of the seemingly trivial and potentially stressful tasks performed each day have the ability to be seen in a new light. I am not suggesting that we don't need limits. Parameters are important—but it is so easy to complain, and it's so easy to try and seek respite, especially from the demanding, ordinary, and often repetitive tasks in life. Believe me; I struggle with these temptations every day. But amidst all the bad news that may swirl around us, amidst all of our daily tasks and responsibilities, we are surrounded with an endless array of God's gifts of grace in the guise of the commonplace. They appear to be routine, but they are remarkable.

These days I try to think of the things I *get* to have on my agenda. You might, as I do, find the mental shift quite amazing. Try it! What tasks or opportunities lie at your feet? Ask yourself, in the middle of your busy life, "What do I *GET* to do?"

Snowsight

Shhhhhh. Go somewhere quiet where you can imagine, and allow your mind to wonder in this story. Sometimes, in the midst of turbulence, comes an unexpected peace. And, sometimes, in the peace, a divine presence can be felt.

The snows that blanketed our area transformed the world around our homes. People rushed to stores, gathered firewood inside their porches, stocked up on provisions, and generally hunkered down for an evening to themselves while their neighborhoods became cloaked in the gathering darkness and the accumulating white powder. I suppose, if you were like me, you might have switched on the front light to check on the mounting snow and marveled at the way it swirled in the wind just inches from the warm sanctuary behind your door. There may have been a fire in your hearth and mugs of hot chocolate sipped. Aside from an intrusive snowplow that punctuated the silence of the night, there was not much else to disturb the hushed conversation and music within the walls of your home. It was a night to surround oneself with comfort, safely harbored away from the elements.

Somewhere well into this very evening, I realized I needed to get something out of my office, not the one in my home, mind you, but the one next door in the church. "Oh well," I thought, "I'll just zip over and be back in a flash. If I run fast enough in my boots, I'll hardly even notice the snow." I bundled up in gloves, boots, coat, and hat and braced myself for my nocturnal passage.

Upon opening the door, I was met with a whirlwind of blown snow and swirling air that made me turn my back toward the door and ease out into the glow of light outside the threshold. My front steps had disappeared, resembling nothing more than a slope that led down to the front yard. Each step brought varying depths of light, dry, snow that had drifted in the gusting wind around my house. Rounding the corner, beyond the range of the glimmering light on my stoop and now immersed in darkness, I noticed that the curb beside the parking lot had vanished, swallowed up by the mounting snow. Before me stretched a vast field of white, animated by curls of wind-lapped snow and lit only by that curious type of light found in a snowstorm. Shades of greys and black mixed and mingled, shadowing and uniting the entire world in its murky glow. A wet coldness began to creep into the top of my boots from the impacted snow, and I thought, as I trudged, which entrance would afford me the best access.

All at once, a sustained blast of air caught me by surprise and awakened my consciousness. There was a heightened sense of awareness that enveloped me, and I found myself tuning into the storm. I was in the middle of a parking lot, but I might as well have been in the middle of Montana rangeland. The world was swirling around me. Driven snow pricked at my face and blinded me for a moment but not for long. Gazing up and peering into the falling snow, I imagined myself hurtling through the Milky Way. I was in New Vernon, but I sensed I was anywhere but there. And from the midst of the buffeting wind came a voice — not one heard by the ears, but in the mind. The immense force of the storm sighed and whispered, "I am God. See what wonders I construct. Lose yourself in Me." I was at once enveloped in God and snow, New Vernon and the wildlands. I was more surrounded by comfort than I had been in my house, yet I was entirely immersed in the elements. My soul could see clearly. I was in myself and out of myself, and I stood still in the wind and frost, just being — arms outstretched, appreciating both the storm and the gift of snowsight.

The gift I was given that night is the one I wish for you. May this year bring you blessings, and may you all find a similar, embracing peace within whatever turbulence rises around you.

The Sounds, Sights, and Knowledge of Christmas

What do your senses experience during the Christmas season? Every year, I try desperately to move beyond the shallow stereotypes of the holiday: countless miles of garland with plastic bows, jolly men in red suits, reindeer, canned music in the malls, presents, and enough candy canes to make every dentist in America leap for joy. I even try to ignore those store-bought, illuminated manger scenes, not to mention the increasing popularity of those inflatable cartoon characters on the front lawns of homes. I try to look deeper. Without a doubt, there is a great deal of substance to be enjoyed during this hopeful, festive time of year, but one needs to simplify one's search to find it and approach this cherished holiday with a heightened sense of awareness. I challenged myself to write a poem on this search. Merry Christmas, my friends!

Morning Glories

What can be heard while crystal breezes drift
Across this still and frozen, silent night?
The secret rip of wrapping creeping down the hall,
The newborn cry of hope upon a fragile world,
And mounting, wish-filled prayers of children in the dark.

What can be seen while flames of candles dance
Behind the frosted windows in the town?
The warmth of family ties rekindled in the glow,
The leaps of joy released from cold and cloistered hearts,
And choirs exhaling angels in the frigid air.

What should be known while all the world awakes
With vines of glory winding through their dreams?
The seeds of faith will flourish in the new-found light,
The blooms of all benevolence grow from the soul,
And those whose prayers are like a child's will find themselves
Fulfilled.

Backwards Vision

*God gave us our memories so that we might
have roses in December.*

~ J. M. Barrie ~

Do I really appreciate Christmas present—as in the here and now? The more years that pass me by, and the more I think about it, I'm beginning to think not. It seems that most of the Christmases from my past, even the ones within the last couple of years, are sweeter in my mind than the one currently passing before my eyes. Maybe it's because I gloss over the reality of the past and fill in the blanks with images that accentuate the best parts of the holiday. It might also be due to the fact that so many of the people that once filled my Christmas mornings just aren't around anymore, and those bittersweet memories makes the yuletides from my younger years seem better. They tap me on my shoulder as if to say, "You didn't know what you had," and perhaps they're right. But, either to escape the pain of their reminders or to fortify my ego, I push them back with thoughts like "oh, well" or "life goes on," as if that might cushion the thorns that come with the blooms of memories.

Did you ever really watch a child approach Christmas? Children divide their time between being forward thinking and being completely immersed in the moment. Gone are the comparisons with the past. Invisible are any "have tos" or pressures to conform to regional expectations for the holiday. Children fully embrace the wonder of the season without batting an eye. They take what they have and build upon it year after year. I used to do this, but at some point during the cycles of the seasons and years, when the undergrowth of life began to crowd my heart, I found my approach changing. I found myself trying more to measure up to some pristine and unrealistic holiday aspiration than making the most out of what was right before my eyes.

Yesterday, I found myself looking through some old photographs. There were a lot of Christmas images: my dad holding me on my brown and white rocking horse, my daughter at five years of age looking wide-eyed at the glistening ornaments on our Christmas tree, and my son joyously petting a donkey in a live nativity. None of them are perfect photos, but they capture the love of the season and embody the magic of the moment. Are there thorns among these roses? Sure…lots of them. My dad and I will never share another Christmas on this earth. My daughter no longer lives at home, and my son, well, he is nearing the age when I first started to look backwards.

But I think, just maybe, I've found an answer. It's okay to have that backwards vision. I just have to put some new faces on it and open my arms and my eyes a little wider. Wide enough to hold my memories for what they are. Wide enough to use them to make new ones. Wide enough to take in and appreciate my world today. Wide enough to capture the true spirit of Christmas unencumbered by the greeting card visions. I want to open my arms as wide as angel wings, as wide as that stable in Bethlehem, and remind myself that those blooms of memory I once had may have passed, but their imagery can become the fertile soil for the blooms of roses I'll treasure *this* December.

May God's love be with you all as we celebrate the birth of the Light unto this world.

His Hands

On December 22, 1992, one week after my father fell back into the arms of God, I sat down to write a poem for his memorial service. I wanted to create something that spoke to the man I knew. I wanted to capture memories, but I also wanted the writing to be from a child's perspective. It was to be the first Christmas without my father in this world, and the more the images of him flooded my mind, the more it dawned on me that the times I had watched my father work, my attention was somehow drawn to his hands. They were the tools that shaped the world around me in that bigger-than-life way that only a father can.

His Hands

I remember his hands
Sticky with the sap from the Christmas tree.
They molded our holiday.
Icy and chapped,
They securely lashed the evergreen to our station wagon.
His hands, powerful and white-knuckled,
Pushed and pulled at the saw,

Which severed a two-inch slice
From the base of the tree.
His hands held the sap-covered offering to my nose.
Scratched and abused,
They withstood the needled assault.
Meticulously,
His hands strung the lights from bough to bough
Like multicolored mountaineers on belay,
Spiraling skyward,
Steadily ascending,
Burning birds of prey
Patiently circling the abundant spoils below.
His hands held lead tinsel,
Which would hang like silver spaghetti
From the spiked, foliated branches.
Honorably,
His hands gingerly placed the time-worn snowman
In its reserved space amongst the branches,
A memory of the hands he recalled.
Delicately,
His hands pierced a bough with the blue, wooden bird.
On Christmas morning
His hands became shells,
Closed tight,
Protecting and concealing its pearl.
Slowly,
They would open and reveal
The traditional, solitary, silver dollar.
During the feast
His hands would busy themselves
Skillfully sharpening, slicing, and serving.

Abruptly,
The routine was dissolved.
His hands refused to perform their yearly maneuvers.
They were absent.
His hands left a void.
The glass mountaineers
And silver spaghetti
Failed to appear.
The snowman lay insulated somewhere in a box of memories.
The absent shells
Removed from our sight
Would now
Slowly open
And grasp the hand of God.

Time, in haste, fills every void.
It is Christmas once again.
Securely, a tree will be tied to an automobile.
Meticulously,
Lights will be strung from bough to bough.
Delicately,
The blue, wooden bird will pierce an evergreen branch.
There will be renewal,
Sharpening, slicing, and serving.
Shells will reveal their silver secret.
I remember,
But I have also learned.
There is now another child to keep watch.
My hands
Will bridge their worlds.

Although he was a stern disciplinarian and had a short temper, as a boy I always imagined my father as someone who knew just about everything. I always liked to measure the size of my hands against my father's — in wet cement, bread dough, mud, beach sand, and palm-on-palm. Even when my hands grew to equal his in size, my father's hands always seemed greater, superior, and more powerful and accomplished in comparison to mine. It was a comparison, I came to realize, which involved the heart and was much more complex than simple measurements of flesh and bone. My father's presence was awesome in my eyes.

I think the relationship we have with God is similar to this. We grow in faith, trusting in and guided by our Heavenly Father, but, in the end, the relationship involves more than just commandments, Bible stories and verses, and holiday rituals; it's about awe. The core of this divine relationship lies in being absolutely floored, dumbstruck, and amazed by our Father's power and beauty. It doesn't take long to realize that any comparison between our creations and those of God's is really no comparison at all. We are surrounded by a world created by God's hands, and we might just want to step back, watch His hands at work, and let them speak to our hearts.

Thank God!

Well, December 25th has come and gone, and I, for one, say, "Thank God!" for more than one reason. When my children were in elementary school, their Christmas concert always ended with the song "Christmas is a Feeling" written by Natalie Sleeth.

> *"For Christmas is a feeling filling the air.*
> *It's love and joy and laughter of people everywhere,*
> *But if Christmas is a feeling bringing such good cheer,*
> *Then why oh why don't you and I*
> *Try to make it last all year?*
> *Why can't it last all year?"*

Every time I hear this song, I have the same reaction. Really? Last all year? Mankind puts up a poor struggle just to make the spirit of Christmas last one night…or maybe one morning of opening gifts, and then it's back to the usual.

Did you experience any Christmas related activity that went awry? I saw people getting into arguments about parking spaces. I witnessed two men almost come to blows while in the checkout line in the grocery store. I heard a person say, "What else do you want for Christmas because I still have more money to spend on you." A couple of individuals were overheard saying they weren't celebrating this year because they didn't see the point in doing so because the decorations come down in a few weeks anyway. Others referred to Christmas as the day when the calendar dictates that we buy things for other people. Shoppers rioted to get bath towels for $1.88 and waffle irons for $2.00, and twenty people were injured after a woman at a Walmart used pepper spray to get an edge on other shoppers in a rush for Xbox game consoles. Have you listened to the expletive-ridden language, which has become commonplace in our society, while you were doing your Christmas shopping? It's akin to those reality television shows where every third word seems to be bleeped out of the audio track, and even a seven year-old could guess what words have been omitted. Ugh!

Charlie Brown asked in 1965, "Isn't there anyone who knows what Christmas is all about?" Ironically, the Grinch alluded to an answer on television in 1966, one animated character to another, when he realized that, "Maybe Christmas, he thought…doesn't come from a store. Maybe Christmas, perhaps…means a little bit more!"

We keep throwing money at Christmas, as if it were going to satisfy us. We keep trying to make our Christmases perfect—the perfect tree, the perfect gift, the perfect meal—but they are futile attempts; it never happened, and it's never going to happen.

The perfect Christmas only happened once. Jesus was born and came to this earth because we are *imperfect*! Mankind hasn't a clue how to do perfection, and it certainly isn't found in bath towels, waffle irons, or Xbox games. Instead, we need to focus on our charge: the responsibility to care for each other and to love each other. It's hard. It's difficult because we need to change our thinking, our actions, and our reactions in order to do that.

My favorite thing to do at Christmas is to take a walk outside at night and realizing that the stars and the moon I see are the same ones Mary and Joseph saw on that first Christmas. It makes me feel very small—the way, I think, Joseph and Mary felt. I'm sure they would have preferred to rest, but Herod was a threat to them. They realized they had to escape in order to save the life of their child. They had to completely change their plans and go far out of their way so that their child could survive, grow, mature, and reinvent eternity.

If Christmas has any chance of lasting all year, it needs to start with our transformation. No one can do it for us. The church can't do it for us. God can't even do it for us. WE, as individuals, have to decide to make a move and realize that we hold the hope for this world in our hearts, much like Joseph and Mary held it in their arms. We need to decide to go out of our way to give love a chance to grow and mature. WE have to change our thinking and plans. WE have to change the way we respond to this world. If we do, God will work wonders through us.

Thank God that Christmas is not about shopping or one night of carols or one day or any present or any meal. It's about love… it's a way of life…it's ongoing…it's about seeing Emmanuel in the eyes of everyone you meet, every day.

Chapter 4
Abide with Me

Love with Patience

How do you come to love God if the relationship with your own father was broken? If you were hurt by your earthly father, how do you bring yourself to trust a heavenly one?

I've thought about these questions and this journey a great deal, largely because my earthly father was often viewed by me as a volatile person whose temper had to be appeased. When it was not, I got hurt. And every time I got hurt, the trust inherent in the parent-child relationship eroded until, eventually, it was reduced to ash.

When I sat in church as a child, I heard the stories, I heard the one-liners, and I heard the directives familiar to many. *Trust in God. God loves you. Put your cares in God's hands. God will protect you. You can confess all of your misdeeds to God, and you will receive forgiveness.* It sounded perfect, but, to me, it also sounded unbelievable and not much more than a shattered fairy tale. Why? I loved my father, but his demeanor turned on a dime. He said he loved me, but the physical and emotional pain he metered out did not reflect his words. I did not feel protected or forgiven. And my father's hands? They were often viewed by me as abusive weapons—not embracive sanctuaries.

It took a very long time for me to trust God because experience had taught me to respond to a father very differently. My emotional scars run deep. I could count on the fact that my father would hit me and scream at me for upsetting him or for even the slightest deviation from his imposed regimen—but trusting him with my feelings and my heart? No, there was never a glimpse of that possibility. As a result, I built a fortification around my heart, and, likewise, I perceived there to be large emotional barriers between God and me.

Trust is a precursor to love, and I couldn't love a God I couldn't trust. God, however, was patient. He loved, and he waited. He loved me. He waited some more. And then he loved me, and he waited. He did this for more than thirty years. Slowly—over time—the walls began to collapse. Little by little, I let down my guard. Bit by bit, I let God inside my heart. And then, one day, the ice around my heart melted on a mountain summit in Maine. I trusted God, and I let God in. His love is amazing, and it is real.

Why am I opening up my soul and telling you this? I want to let you know that love, sometimes, takes time. I want to let you know that we shouldn't give up on loving each other. Some of us have been so broken that we need time to rebuild our hearts. Sometimes God's love needs to chip away at our hearts, and sometimes we need to love each other gently but consistently without expecting anything in return. Some of us need reassurance, and sometimes the best gift we can give someone for whom we care is the gift of time, within which are planted the seeds of trust.

God offers His love to all of us. Deep in the depths of our hearts are the seeds of trust and His love. Some sprout immediately. Some take years to germinate. Nurture these seeds in each other. Do not give up! Reassure. Love with patience. Reassure. Love with patience. Reassure. Love with patience. In time, love will take hold. Eventually, love will conquer both doubt and fear. Dare to love gently and consistently without losing faith. Let God's love flow through you and into the hearts of those around you. Be patient. For the unwavering warmth of our Heavenly Father's love will melt even the most cloistered of hearts.

Typographical Error

I write all the time. E-mails, essays, letters, manuscripts, poems, speeches, prayers, songs, Dear sir, Dear madam, To Whom It May Concern, Dear Mr. or Mrs. Whoever-You-Might-Be…I've written it all. When it's good, it flows out of me without effort, an amazing feeling that puts me in a timeless zone and leaves me feeling exhilarated at the finish, not unlike a good run. I've always held fast to the belief that I am only the conduit, and it isn't really me doing the writing; it's something inside of me, perhaps outside of me, that comes up with the words, flowing out of me like a stream fed by a spring with a mysterious source. Like any spring, there are concerns that it may one day run dry, but so far it has not. Good or bad, the words keep coming.

And so it was on one day in late autumn that I sat down to type a response to one of my friends. Errors—typographical errors—are not things I worry about when I write first drafts. I hold fast to the premise established in Ernest Kurtz's and Katherine Ketcham's book *The Spirituality of Imperfection*. Basically, it states that man is by nature imperfect. If one embraces this truth, then we begin to look at our actions in a new light. When we make mistakes, we are actually reaffirming this premise by acting as perfect human beings. Therefore, we need to cut ourselves some slack and stop expecting perfection out of ourselves, beings with imperfect wiring. This has a great impact on writing, an art that demands drafts, many of them, before reaching a finished product. Accepting this belief, I wait until I have my ideas set on paper before I even begin to consider editing and rearranging my thoughts. There are many corrections to ponder, but spelling is one of the last things I check. Yes, I admit it; spellcheck is one of my best friends, although, as most of us know, even this is fallible.

Getting back to my letter… The communication I was typing to my friend was written, revised a couple of times, spellchecked, and then sent off into cyberspace by way of my computer. That evening I received a response.

"What did you mean by starting the letter with God?" my friend wrote. "It's clever!"

I had no idea what he meant…none at all. I didn't remember mentioning God anywhere.

"What are you talking about?" I E-mailed in return.

"Look in the greeting," he responded.

I checked, and there it was, a typographical error, a slip of the finger, a mistake…or was it? I had intended to write Good Morning! But that's not what I wrote. I typed *God Morning!* And it made me pause, for so it was. It was God's morning, and, oblivious as I was to the whole event, He had been working through me, moving my fingers, communicating through my keyboard without my knowledge, creating this "mistake." It was the "spirituality of imperfection" made tangible. It was the Perfect working through the imperfect. I loved this moment!

Now, think about this for a few minutes. How many times have we all said, "good morning?" We say it without thinking. We say it without pause. We say it without meaning, expectations, or cause. BUT, what if we omit one little letter, what of it then? Well, we have a whole different animal, you see. Have you heard the response to our greeting, "What's so good about it?" Now we have an answer, and it lies in the essence of the morning's very creation. It's a good morning because it is God's morning. It's a new day given to us to do His work, to love one another as He loved us, to see the world as a glass half-full and not half empty, to know that we have the power to make a difference, even if it's for those few people we greet at the dawn of the new day.

So...I say, "God Morning to you all! How might you use this day that God has given to you and the rest of the world?" I'm going to keep this greeting in mind as I get my family going in the morning and head out of my home. Perhaps you might do the same. Try it in your house of worship, on the train, in the office, wherever you might happen to be. Be ready for some quizzical looks, but you'll have the perfect justification for your exclamation. Who knows? We could start a God Morning trend that could spread out into the larger world, increase people's awareness of God, and create another way to weave faith into our daily lives.

And in the evening...while we're at it...when our day is finished, when we switch off the lights...let's whisper to those we love..."God Night."

Proof

The heavens declare the glory of God: and the firmament proclaims His handiwork.

~ Psalm 19:1 ~

What proof do you need that God exists? No...really...what would it truly take to seal the deal for you? For anyone? We live in such a tangible, materialistic world where the burden of proof is often just that—a burden. Our ancestors lived in a much different time, a time of belief in a variety of things good and evil. Thankfully, those superstitious beliefs have disappeared, but what about God? In the wake of the supremacy of science and technology, what casualties have our beliefs in God suffered?

We live in a "show me," bait-and-switch culture. In A Christmas Carol, Scrooge says, "I don't ship until I have the cash in hand." Sound familiar? Spin doctors bend reality to fit their desired outcomes and goals. Conspiracy theories abound on so many issues appearing to be open-and-shut cases that it seems as if nothing is safe from being questioned, even those events witnessed by many people. Seriously, if people can be convinced that Elvis is still alive, how are we supposed to present enough evidence to prove that God exists?

One of the best responses I've heard to this question has to do with the apostles. It's been documented that these men existed, and it's also documented that almost all of them were martyred for their Christian beliefs. As a result, some of the best convincing evidence is found in the question, "Why would these men go to their deaths for something that wasn't real?"

Others point out the window and into the heavens. Similar to the quote from Psalm 19, there are those who say that the world around us and the seemingly infinite stars above our heads is proof that there is a God, an intelligent designer at work. Can you think of other reasons that may prove there is a God…any God? I'm sure you can, but for every single reason, there are going to be people who disagree. Perhaps that's just human nature. Maybe there's something in us that can't turn away from a mystery, even if it's one we feel a need to create.

Look, for some of us, an ungrounded belief comes all too quickly. I'm reminded of a television commercial I once saw that features a woman who brags about dating a French model. How does she know he's a French model? Well, she read his bio on the Internet, and anything on the Internet has to be true! Hopefully, you don't believe that, but it goes to show that there's a great deal of latitude out there when it comes to standards for faith.

In a world of superstitious beliefs, ethereal demons, and imagined incantations an intangible God was easily accepted as an appropriate defense. Nowadays, with nuclear weapons, virulent strains of viruses we can see under a microscope, random shooters arbitrarily blowing away innocent victims, and more, some would say an intangible God is not enough protection and doesn't supply a sufficient insurance policy for them. Real fears demand a real God, a materialistic defense.

You know what? Hogwash! Maybe, come to think of it, our ancestors had it easier when it comes to believing in God. Maybe faith needs to be exempted from the burden of proof. I don't want a tangible deity. I don't want quantitative proof of God. The moment you quantify something, you limit it. I, for one, don't want to put my God in a box. I Am is exactly the kind of God I want...with no name...with no limitations...because that kind of God can do anything.

My father used to say that faith in God was a crutch. That was before he got sick and his age brought wisdom. Eventually, God was all-important and filled his days and nights. In my father's last years, his Father was the most important thing in his life. Believe me—that was about as radical a change as one could hope to witness. But, hey, if someone wants to convince me that God doesn't exist, I say the burden of proof is on his or her shoulders. I have my real, intangible faith in my unquantifiable God, and that's all the proof I need.

Dividing Walls

Something there is that doesn't love a wall.
~ Robert Frost, "Mending Wall" ~

I am continually aware of the signature of man upon the landscape. During a visit to the Robert Frost cabin in Ripton, Vermont, I strolled up the wooded lane that leads to his former home. Threading their ways through the maple trees and along the grass-laden fields are grey, stone fences, hedgerows that had been built by farmers and property owners over the years. This honor guard of stones are now no longer neatly stacked but lay scattered and toppled in haphazard piles of varying heights and widths, the victims of weathering, freezing, thawing, and heaving ground. These were not the walls that originally inspired Frost to write his famous poem, "Mending Wall," but I could better understand why they impressed him, and I also realized something else. Robert Frost was spot-on correct. There *is* something that doesn't love a wall, but the poet never says what it is. I know for a fact that it's not people.

People fill their world with walls. We build them all the time. They come in all sizes and shapes. There are little walls, like the ones we build in our gardens. There are big walls like the Great Wall of China. (This one can even be seen from space!) What material would you like to use to build your wall? We have stone, brick, sheetrock, wood, plastic, steel, stucco, cinder block, and more. Walls are not your cup of tea? Build a fence! We have them, too. We fence in our yards, our gardens, our pets, and our livestock. We even learn at a very early age that walls and fences are a part of life from our mothers and fathers. Ever meet modern parents who don't have a baby gate or a playpen? Nope...me either.

Not enough separation for you? Humans work in cubicles and in offices. Our homes have walls to make rooms for cooking, reading, sleeping, washing, eating, and entertaining. We worry about who's crossing our national borders, transporting materials over state lines, and the municipal codes for fences facing the street. There are even walls we can't see. We all have them. They surround our personal space. Try talking too close to someone's face or sitting right next to a stranger in an empty movie theater, and you'll see what I mean.

Walls are an inescapable feature in our physical lives, and we would be hard pressed to imagine life without them, but that's exactly what God commands us to do. Can we follow His command? I honestly don't know if we're up to the challenge. We have a hard enough time just managing the walls between us and God, let alone ourselves. Besides, where would we start?

I think we need to begin by moving out of our comfort zone. Start doing little things that stretch our normal, learned manner of behavior. What about that clerk across the counter from you? You see her every morning when you buy coffee. Did you ever introduce yourself, ask her name, or strike up a conversation about something relevant to both of you? Yeah, I know, it's not something I always think about either. Sadly, I often think I'm too busy going where I need to go to strike up a conversation. Well, then, how about that delivery person who brings the packages to your home or office? Did you ever ask him about his life, something small to break the ice? Then there's that utility repair crew...know anything about them? What about something even easier. Take a look at the person with whom you ride the train every day for thirty minutes or more. There are people who may spend more time in our presence than some family members, yet we don't even know their names. What would you say to them?

The key to Kingdom of God living is getting out of our own skin, and that's hard...really hard...but not impossible. It takes effort to live a life with fewer walls, but it can begin with the smallest, well placed act of community building at a fundamental level. Shake a hand, buy a cup of tea, or say "How are you?" and mean it by waiting for a reply. Look for God in the eyes of a stranger, behind the sunglasses, behind the different eye color, beyond the unfamiliarity of unique appearance or customs. Do you see Him? There He is!

Stones in walls never stack themselves; we have to decide to do the stacking. And even the most well-built walls will topple if their foundations are weakened. Hey, I know some walls around our own towns that are ready to come down. Anybody want to lend a hand?

God of Child

Have you ever looked at a child with amazement? More specifically, have you ever looked at a child and been shown a glimpse of the Eternal? You may have found it in the inflection of the voice, a glint in the eye, or an action or gesture that transcended childhood and made you aware of the sacred essence inside us all. It also makes us acutely aware of the precious nature of time and of the crucial importance of our position as adult role models in the lives of children. The following poem expresses how I found my glimpse one day, and without warning, in my own son. These moments are there for all of us to see in all children, and I urge each of you to look for it in a child that you know. Go and search in peace.

God of Child

When I reached out and touched the hand that brushed
    sleep from my morning eyes,
I saw Your love incarnate sitting on my pillow,
Smiling, goodness, inches from my face.
And I gave thanks, for I could feel, and I could hear, and I
    could turn to greet and see
You in my little child, who said, "Can we have pancakes
    now?"
Though it was Your voice all along.
So up we rose like blazing suns and spent our clattering
    pan and syrup hour
Raking in the breath of life, too potent, raw, ambrosial,
    energetic,
Pikes of light that pierce the soul and linger in the mind
Like pinwheels whirling in the breeze of some enchanted
    land.
But this is here, and You sit cross-legged on my carpet
    looking up at me
Through eyes of five year's worth of life, yet wise enough
    to know the genesis of stars.
And so it goes throughout the day, each step a dance,
Each thought a novel of experience that far outweighs the
    moments we retain.

Tripping to the market even seems like paradise.

You hold my hand to cross the crowded lot and say,
"Daddy, can we go to the bakery?"

And so it turns, morning into afternoon, smiling, flying

Frisbees, running races up the drive,

Skinning hands, Bactine and Bacitracin blunders, but

Your voice cries, "Ouch, it hurts! Make it better!" and soon
I kiss the tears away.

We settle in for supper. Sleepy-eyed, You eat strawberries
from a bowl and start to think

And glance at me as if to say, "You are my world." My
jammied, tooth-brushed child

Who climbs into the bed and begs for *Gwendolyn the Miracle
Hen.* "Just one more time?"

And so we read and listen to the weary pages crumple as
they turn

Until the metered sound

Is mixed with rhythmic breaths…

You drift off to Your world, and leave me with my child,

An angel vessel living through Your life.

And I know I would die for this and wonder at the parallel,

For as I would for my own child, so You have done for all
of us,

For as my child would ask and look to me, so we beseech
and trust in You.

And as I watch my dear one dream, I feel the tug of sleep I
can't resist

And fall away to fly

Like rising moons with You and mine, inches from my face,

Hand in hand and soaring on the nexus of Your endless
love,

Enveloped in the gentle and enduring palm of heaven.

Eulogy

Lately, I've been thinking of moving. When you live in a place for long enough, you accumulate memories of houses and the people who live in them. As time progresses, we find that some people still reside in the same homes we remember, while some have moved on.

My friend Garrett and I met as a result of a book I wrote called *A Bit of Earth*, which reveals the layers of history around Bernardsville, New Jersey. It's where I grew up, and it's a place where Garrett also spent part of his youth. It turns out that he lived in the same house that was previously owned by my godparents. As if that wasn't enough to pique Garrett's interest, the last chapter in the book details the paranormal events that have occurred in the area's houses and general vicinity. Well... history, Bernardsville, and ghosts proved to be an irresistible combination for Garrett. He contacted me not long after the book was published, and we became good friends — to the point where I even had the honor of becoming his daughter's godfather. The subsequent five years were somewhat of a roller coaster ride filled with all sorts of memories.

During several weeks after his passing, I had been recalling my memories of Garrett, and even gone back to walk up and down Lloyd Road, recalling the pasts of two boys that overlapped in the same place but at different times. We found a number of things that Garrett and I shared in common, including an interest in the Revolutionary War and the historical places around our homes. Morristown National Historical Park and the Wallace House in Somerville were places he especially enjoyed visiting, as was the Prallsville Mills section of Stockton, NJ. Garrett had a fascination with George Washington, one which resulted in a collection of books, artwork, and original documents from Washington's era. He loved it and was proud of it.

On several occasions, Garrett, my son Cory, and our friend Joe would find time to go fishing at a private pond along Hardscrabble Road in Bernardsville. One summer, Garrett had a very successful day with us, catching several bass and a trout. Standing on the sun-drenched dock, line in the water, one would think he didn't have a care in the world. He had a great time that day, and I understand his fish ended up tasting pretty good, too. Often after fishing, we'd drive down the road to the Grain House restaurant for dinner and a beer. Garrett and Joe would order steaks and burgers, while I suffered continual ribbing from Garrett for my "girly" order of hummus and pita bread.

Ghosts also intrigued Garrett. Along with Al Rauber, we became the three, lead members of Haunted New Jersey. We investigated many sites together, including the Merchant's House Museum and Jockey Hollow. Garrett always favored skeptical research, and his expertise as a computer forensic examiner lent itself perfectly to our efforts to collect audio evidence at the sites we visited. Eventually, at his suggestion, our efforts led to a book about several, historic, haunted sites in central New Jersey. As a result, Garrett and I also lectured together on occasion.

However, the memories that stand out foremost in my mind are centered on our Haunted New Jersey podcasts. One of Garrett's catch phrases to begin the show was "Hey! What's going on?" With guests and friends such as Dan, Jenn, Chris, and others, Garrett recorded and produced podcasts that were informative, level-headed, and always very amusing, tinged with his special brand of humor. He enjoyed playing EVPs on the show. EVP stands for Electronic Voice Phenomena, recordings of anomalous voices that aren't heard at the time of the recording. Are they from the other side? No one is sure, but they are intelligent, meaning they respond directly to questions. The phenomenon is being studied by NASA and other groups, and it proved to be quite an interesting area of study for Garrett. We played many of these recordings on the show, but my favorite EVP captured by Garrett is a male voice that says, "I have seen God."

The gifts of time and experiences that all of us shared with Garrett make me keenly aware of a larger gift of awareness. As is often the case, I now look back on those times and events with Garrett, wishing I could freeze time, but we all know that isn't possible. However, having our recollections of Garrett and an awareness of these shadows from our pasts means we can always keep him close to us.

Garrett's condition and his battles with his personal demons prepared me for the news I received on the evening of April 30th, and here's where the thoughts of moving come into focus. Moving is change, and change happens all the time. In many ways, the death of the body is similar to moving. We leave these earthly houses, these bodies, these shells behind because they no longer fit us or serve us properly. We're ready for something better. Sometimes houses fall apart, and the people inside are forced to move. Garrett's his mind and body could not sustain him any longer.

Life prepares us for understanding this transition by providing a seemingly endless list of examples. A butterfly leaves a chrysalis. A hermit crab abandons a shell for a larger one. We cover ourselves with garments and change our clothes. We go to school and change classes. We change schools. We graduate and move on to our careers, which most of us change several times. We change phases of life, addresses, towns, cars, groups of friends—the list goes on and on. We leave things behind in all of these instances, while we move on to something better or more appropriate…or more safe and healthy. God doesn't set us up to learn about recurring patterns of metamorphosis and change in this life only to pull the rug out from us at *our* time of transition.

Do you know the difference between a house and a home? A house becomes a home only when people live inside it. A house surrounds them. We don't miss the houses we knew from our childhoods; we miss the people who lived inside them. I think we're like those Russian nesting dolls. You know…those hollow, wooden dolls that fit inside each other. I've always thought that the most precious nesting doll was the one inside all the other larger ones. Likewise, all of us live inside a body found inside of clothes found inside of houses or cars, office buildings, stores, schools, and houses of worship. There is an essence in all of our earthly shells that has a role to play. And when that role is complete, when we learn what we need to learn and achieve what we are supposed to achieve and touch the lives of those we need to impact, or our bodies and minds give out, we move away, and we graduate to God. It is as simple and amazing and wonderful as that.

Do not mourn any of our passed loved ones as dead; they have simply moved. They have left their physical bodies behind, ones that no longer served them. The inner, most precious nesting dolls that are the real individuals with whom we fell in love and knew as a husband, father, family member, or friend escaped to a new existence and still live.

I like to imagine how peaceful Garrett and the rest of our loved ones are right now, for they can now say of themselves, "I have seen God." They have discovered how they can still speak to our hearts, and they have found that there will come a time when they can once again be with us all, free of the challenges that faced them in this life.

Now it's up to us to hold up our end of this new relationship, and it comes with a couple of hopes for us.

Number 1: May we keep all of our friends and loved ones who have passed in the present tense. Try not to say anyone was. He or she *IS!*

Number 2: May we forgive the mistakes and misdeeds of the past and keep the gifts that these people gave us close to our hearts and be aware of how those who have passed are still touching our lives. There are signs of them all around us.

Celebrate their graduation—their transition, their move. Be happy for the tranquility that now surrounds them and know that there will be a time when our spirits will join again, when we also become fully aware of eternity, and fall back into the arms of God. Until then... You can speak to any of your departed loved ones; they will immediately hear. You can remember, and they will be with you instantly. Hold them in your heart and soul, and you will be inseparable.

Celebrate their spiritual life, for they are no longer limited by a physical body and mind. They are alive in spirit, and they are well. In some ways, he or she *is* and *will be* with us all—now more than ever—perhaps *better* able and more free to commune with the part inside all of us that is eternal and belongs to God. And so, when all of us are finished with this Earth, may we all have this similar experience. I know that when my work here is complete, and I make the transition from this life to the next and find myself surrounded with friends and relatives who made the journey before me, somewhere in that encircling chorus of voices I will recognize a particularly friendly greeting, one that's saying, "Hey! What's going on?"

Made New

When my daughter Melina was very young, we used to delight in going for bicycle rides. I would buckle her into her bike seat, put on her helmet, and away we'd go! These rides were not short, round-the-block types of jaunts. These were lengthy excursions of twelve to fifteen miles. Melina used to love holding her arms and hands out during the rides and pretend she was a bird in flight, and I would find humor in making her laugh by riding over bumps in the road. To Melina, I was just about the most amazing thing she could imagine in the world—a view, I suppose, that most children have of their fathers. To me, Melina was, and is, my world.

Melina would made me laugh with her childish interpretations of her environment, and I got to see the most mundane and cliché events and expressions made new through her young eyes. One of her interpretations occurred on one of our bike trips. We were riding on Peachcroft Road in Bernardsville, NJ, on a very warm day. Peachcroft is a long, serpentine road that seems even longer if one is riding *up* its hill steep hill, which we were. Do you know the expression, "strong as an ox?" It makes sense to an adult because we appreciate the strength of this muscular, bovine mammal. To Melina, however, this phrase carried with it absolutely no sense of the strength of this animal. She simply thought that one could insert any animal's name into the phrase, and it could be given and accepted as a compliment. So there we were with me peddling up the hill, sweating, inhaling rhythmic gulps of air, getting thirsty, and occasionally rising out of the saddle to ease the climb. All Melina had to do was amuse herself and listen to her father grunt his way up the incline. Perceptive of my efforts, she chose the most exhausting part of the hill to offer me her words of encouragement. She reached out, tapped me on the small of my back, and said, "You can do it, Dad. You're as strong as a duck."

I laughed. I laughed so hard that I had to stop peddling. Suddenly, the exhaustion vanished, the hill no longer mattered, and I wasn't thirsty. All I felt was happiness and an overwhelming love for my daughter as she sat smiling at me from under her bike helmet. The moment was perfect. Up until that event, I had travelled up Peachcroft Road more times than I can remember by car, bike, or on foot with no significant memories to show for them, but now this road reminds me only of that experience with Melina. The old had become new.

In January, we begin a new year, and the month is often seen as a new opportunity to start fresh and begin anew. The same can be said for our relationship with God, except that we don't have to wait for New Year's Day. We can start at any point and at any time because, through our Creator, all things become new, the old is washed away. Our faith in God and our relationship with Him makes even the most difficult things easier. Feel His presence. Listen for His words of comfort and encouragement. We may be strong, perhaps, if we're lucky, even as strong as ducks, but nothing compares to the strength found in our Creator.

Shutters

*"Why don't you think of [God] as the one who is coming,
who has been approaching from all eternity...
the ultimate fruit of a tree whose leaves we are."*

~ Rainer Maria Rilke, "Letters to a Young Poet" ~

I know a small, historic church whose simple yet beautiful sanctuary was graced with gorgeous arched windows that seemed to reach up to heaven. They dated from the early nineteenth century, and their individual panes of glass bore the quaint, wavy patterns indicative of blown glass. On the interior side of the windows were exquisitely handcrafted shutters, which were permanently affixed in such a manner so that less than fifty percent of their total area could be completely folded back from the windows.

Over time, these windows and shutters began to show their age, and eventually reached the point where repair of individual window panes was nearly impossible without damaging the mullions. The shutters, too, had become difficult to close and were heavy with many coats of paint. A decision was made to have the windows and shutters rebuilt or repaired with historical accuracy. The process was long and expensive, but when the new windows were finally installed, the entire congregation marvelled at the way the lacework of window panes let in the bright light of the day. After all, none of the members could remember a time when there weren't shutters on their church windows.

The sanctuary had never been more brilliant. The panes of glass were now fully unencumbered and remained free of any covering... until two months later when the flawless, restored shutters were reinstalled, in accordance with the historic design of the church. Now, while the shutters were stunning in appearance, some people remarked on what a shame it was that the artistry of the windows, especially that of the top arches, was now blocked from view by the shutters. What's more, the brilliant light, which had, for eight weeks, been allowed to stream into the sanctuary, was now blocked from entry.

It wasn't that the people disliked the fresh, white, wooden shutters; they were beautiful and aesthetically pleasing in their own right. They missed the abundant light and window design that they had never had the opportunity to experience beforehand. Their eyes had been opened to a new appreciation and a new way of perceiving. You see, there is always compromise when things meet and combine, and there is an obvious question posed and, often, overlooked when the use of shutters is employed. What becomes of the light?

Consider our hearts and the way we open ourselves up or draw our shutters to the light of our Creator. The shutters on people's hearts differ from the ones found on windows, for they hold no aesthetic beauty. They are strictly functional. Some people are very open to God, allowing the divine light to shine fully on them and all they do. Others are content to know that God is out there, even joyful about God's existence, but content to let the Divine remain outside. In effect, many people block out the light of the Eternal by placing shutters over their hearts. Oh, they certainly have faith, to varying degrees, but only allow portions of their minds and actions to reflect their faith. They don't allow the light of God to flood throughout their entire lives and beings.

Shutters on windows serve a purpose, keeping some desired things in and other unwelcome things out. If they're on the outside, they can provide a defensive barrier to protect the fragile windows from rain, wind, and storm damage. Shutters help to keep internal heat from escaping as easily through the thin panes of glass. Furthermore, shutters keep the damaging rays of the sun from fading interior fabrics and surfaces.

However, the metaphorical shutters found on some people's hearts block out a different kind of light, a light that we need to live fully and be immersed in joy and love. Keeping the divine light out of our hearts hinders us. This light doesn't fade us; it strengthens and rejuvenates. It energizes and invigorates us. It inspires us to live in ways we couldn't imagine without its influence.

Plus, I'll share a fact that some of you already know. This light of God that some people try to avoid, or at least conceal, it's tenacious. Unlike the light of day, God's light is always there. It never goes away. It knows no night time. It knows no darkness it cannot purge. There is no sorrow it cannot vanquish. There is no storm it cannot overcome. And there is no place it cannot reach…even the shadowy recesses of the darkest human heart. In fact, the only thing people have to fear from this divine light is keeping it out of their lives.

So, go ahead. Open your shutters. Open them wide. Take this opportunity to experience and see a different kind of radiance, one you may not have fully experienced, one that feeds your soul. Allow this light of love into your life, a light that, as the poet says, "has been approaching from all eternity." You'll be astonished by the brilliance you let into your world.

Beautiful Mess

How broken are you? No, seriously, how imperfect are you? How messy is your life? Notice that I didn't ask *if* you were broken or imperfect or *if* your life was messy. I asked how much. When you look in the mirror, do you see flaws in your appearance? When you interact with others, do you wish you could change some of your behaviors? Perhaps even more interestingly, when you are all alone, are you aware of thought patterns or feelings that just don't feel right? It's really not a question about whether we are flawed as individuals, for we all are. It's really all about taking a detailed look at the flaws that we own as ourselves.

When I think about myself, there isn't one thing—even among the things I excel at doing—that I do perfectly. I don't write, I don't love, I don't see, teach, or lead others perfectly. There's always room for improvement. If you think about that too much, it can get depressing because it quickly becomes very apparent how messy we really are. By now, you may be feeling a bit anxious or want to stop reading. But wait! I have good news! What if all of our mistakes, all of our messes, and all of the things about ourselves that we label as flaws are part of being a perfect human being? What?! How can someone be perfect and flawed at the same time? The answer lies in the fact that we are human. That's right! You see, if humans are, by nature, imperfect, then our mistakes and flaws stand as testimonies to the fact that we are living our lives as perfect human beings.

I have to remind myself of this all the time. I'm one of those people who don't like to forgive myself for anything. My conscience is a stern taskmaster, and I spend a good deal of time beating myself up for things that happened yesterday, last month, and even many years ago. However, God knows I'm not perfect. In fact, God made me imperfect. This doesn't mean that we shouldn't aspire to improve. To the contrary, trying to live lives with integrity, love, forgiveness, and kindness is a good thing, but we can't maintain it. We're simply not wired to do that. We will constantly and most assuredly stray from our moral aspirations, and, for the most part, we'll continue to feel badly when this occurs. But maybe we need to give ourselves a break and lean on our Creator a little bit more.

Do you ever spiral emotionally? Do you get so caught up in punishing yourself that you end up in a place where the mental anguish greatly outweighs the transgression? When I do this, I try to remember that God knows my heart, loves me, accepts me, and forgives me. If God can forgive me, I guess it's okay to self-forgive as well. God knows our mistakes. He knows how utterly broken we all are, whether it be in our actions, our words, or our hearts. We are God's children—God's creations. Our mistakes and our flaws are known to God before we even make or recognize them, yet He loves us anyway. If you're a parent, you understand. We know our children will act in certain ways and make mistakes and poor judgments, sometimes before they even take place, but we continue to love them. There's nothing that will change or diminish a parent's love. It's the same way with God and all of us.

At any time of year, but especially in spring, the time of rebirth, remember how we are loved by God, just as we are. During the times when we find it hard to forgive ourselves, may we remember that we are children of God. When things get messy and out of control, when you begin to spiral, remember that you are beautiful in God's eyes. God doesn't love or expect our perfection because we will never attain the quality of perfection as humans. He knows that because He made us. No, our Creator loves us despite our flaws and with all our quirks and mistakes. God loves us in our human skin—His children, each of us perfect by virtue of the fact that we are imperfect. We are each a special creation, a beloved and beautiful mess.

The Persistence of God

"What was that?" I asked.

"I said, if I didn't know better, I'd say it looks like snow. Hi, I'm Vince," said the unassuming character who sat next to me at the auto care shop.

Vince was fifty-eight years old, portly, with semi-long salt-and pepper hair, a moustache, and a beard. His plaid shirt, work pants, Carhartt jacket, and steel-toed boots told me he was used to the physical side of life, but he had a warm smile and a personable demeanour to him.

"Yep, the older I get, the more I can't stand the cold," he quipped. "I've broken more bones than I care to remember. I've fallen three times for a total of one hundred feet. The worst one was several years ago while I was huntin' one day up behind my farm in Long Valley. I had forty-five acres of woods behind my home, and I set out before light for my favorite tree stand.

I packed me a big lunch, but," he said with a wink, "I ate it all before 6:00 in the morning. There was nothin' much happenin', so I set back to rest, and before I knew it, I was asleep. Now, I had a safety railing around my stand, which works, as long as you're standin', but I was sittin' down, so the railing was above my head. Don't you know? I fell off that stand while I was sleepin'...broke both of my arms in three places, broke my left femur, and suffered internal injuries. There was nobody around cuz I like to hunt alone, and nobody knew where I was or what I was doin'. I couldn't move. I jus' lay there wonderin' what I was gonna do. The pain was bad, like nothin' I'd ever had before."

"What did you do? Did someone find you?" I asked.

"After layin' there on the ground for what I guess was four hours, I heard a voice. God talked to me...said to use my cell phone. I didn't do it. In fact, I argued with God for about six hours cuz I knew that phones don't work up there. I can get reception at the end of my farm's driveway, but that's it. After, like I said, about six hours, it started to freezin' rain, and it was starting to get dark, and God kept tellin' me, "Use your phone. Use your phone." He was persistent, so I decided I'd try it. Remember, both of my arms were broken in three places, and I hurt a lot, so it took me about an hour for me to move my arm to the point where I could reach my phone. You know what? It worked. I got through and got help. They had to airlift me outta there, but I don't remember much after the call. Well, I gotta tell you. That phone never worked up there before my accident, and I've gone back a few times afterwards. There's never any signal at all, but for some reason, it worked that day when God told me to call."

"That's an amazing story," I said, now completely wrapped up in Vince's tale. "Do you still have the farm?"

"No... I lost it. My farm was worth several million dollars, but I had too many bills. I went through a divorce six years ago, and I got diabetes and cancer. I was on chemo for 2 years—sick as a dog, and I couldn't work. The government put liens on everything I had. I'm several million dollars in debt. I get all my food from food stamps and a soup kitchen. But I've had a good life. I've owned some amazing houses. I sold one of my homes to the King of Morocco. It just sold for nine million dollars. I was friends with Mike Tyson when he lived in Bernardsville. I knew Malcolm Forbes…used to ride my bike with him…and I've hunted big game all over the world, so I can't complain. God's been very good to me. I worship in a church in Sayreville. Love it. Wouldn't trade it for anything. God saved my life once, so I want to praise Him for as long as I live."

With that, my car was ready. The oil was changed and the tires were rotated. As I stood at the counter, Vince got up and walked over to me and looked me in the eye. "Thanks for listening," he said.

"No…thank you!" I responded. "You have strengthened my faith in God and mankind today. Some people would think you have every reason in the world to be angry at God and abandon him, but you didn't."

We shook hands, smiled, and I walked out to my car, thinking how much I have for which to be thankful. Most of the time, I don't see it. I don't realize it. I don't think about it. Vince had reminded me that status quo isn't permanent. There are no guarantees of anything except one thing. Wherever we are, God loves us and cares for us, and we should show him our love in return. That's the most important thing we need to remember… ever.

The Habit of Becoming

I got married in October, 2010. When one contemplates marriage in mid-life, there's an "eyes wide open" character that accompanies the decision. I was set in my ways. I battled memories and fears of what occurred in the past, determined not to encounter them again. I surrounded myself with walls, for emotional defense, which were very hard to breach. Fortunately, with my fiancée's help, those walls have crumbled. I have found joy, and I now compare my current emotional state with that of even a year ago and wonder at how blind I was. What was I thinking? How much time did I waste while the answer to my heart was in front of me for almost ten years?

On a Sunday morning in April, I was walking from the sanctuary to the Fellowship Hall of church, and I became privy to a conversation that two cyclists were having while riding up the road, about twenty feet to my left. One rider was addressing his struggles with maintaining his weight, and he commented on a particular solution he had found for staying slim.

> I thought that if I ate correctly and kept my weight down long enough, I would get used to being thin, and then it wouldn't be a struggle anymore. Thin would become normal for me. It worked! I became a thin man, not just a man who was thin sometimes.

That statement struck me as being applicable to many facets of life, not the least of which is our relationship with God, and I could surely see how it applied to my life. Aren't we all more or less set in our ways? Don't we all have fears of what may occur in the future? Haven't we all constructed walls between ourselves and God? I know my responses to these questions are: I am, I do, and I have. Perhaps, if people got used to spending time with God, they would become spiritually-centered individuals, not just people who thought of God sometimes.

We all develop habits, occasionally without being conscious of them, which keep us apart from God. It might be lack of prayer, spotty attendance at worship services, or just not allowing time to hear that voice of God speak to us. What would happen if we worked at letting go of those habits? God could change our hearts and fill them with new habits, ones that are better for us.

We all have fears and memories of pain and suffering in our lives. We may have even blamed God for those times, and we may have come to a place where we no longer trust God. Perhaps if we dare to lay our fears aside, we will experience God filling our lives with love and strength for the challenges we face.

We all have emotional walls, sometimes even complete fortresses, which we have built around our hearts. Yes, they do a good job of keeping out the things that might hurt us, but take another look. They also act as barriers for the elements in life that have the potential to bring us tremendous joy. Try letting the walls crack and crumble and trust that God will allow joy to enter your life.

God meant for our lives to be lived fully, without fear and without walls, but sometimes our habits and defenses interfere with that plan. In a way, we cheat ourselves out of the joy of communion with God. So, here's a challenge for you. Redesign the cyclist's solution and try this thought on for size.

> If I open my heart to my heavenly father, I will get used to being a child of God, and then it won't be a struggle anymore. Communing with God will become normal for me. It can work! I can become a God-centered person, not just someone who thinks of God sometimes.

Out of the Deep

My friend, Kelley, shared a story with me about a whale watch trip she took in Hawaii. If you have experienced the sighting of whales, then you know the unique feeling you get when you encounter these behemoths of our oceans.

Whales are wild. They're not trained. Sometimes they show up, and sometimes they don't, but they're always out there below the surface of the waves. On an average whale watch excursion, I would guess that people get to see a handful of these magnificent creatures, and some companies even guarantee sightings. Kelley was extremely fortunate on her trip. She went out with a non-profit research/preservation group, rather than a commercial company, and estimates their group must have seen 80-100 whales! In addition, her group saw at least ten, full, out-of-the-water breaches! Even the crew exclaimed that, on a scale of 1 to 10, this particular trip was a 27!

The crew members were actually scrambling for *their* cameras when this enormous Humpback whale started "playing" with the boat! The law requires that boats stay at least one hundred yards away from any whales. Problem is, no one told this whale! In cases where these gentle giants wander in near a boat, the crew is required to shut down the engines and wait for the whale to move on and away from the boat. On Kelley's trip, a huge (and she emphasizes HUGE) fellow surfaced about two feet from the side of the boat during the return trip. It then proceeded to go under the boat and come up on the other side and continue doing so, back-and-forth and back-and-forth, pleasantly holding the watchers "hostage" for at least an extra half hour with an absolutely amazing display!

Needless to say, Kelley arrived back in port a changed woman. There's something deep inside all of us that is touched when we experience communion with another creature, especially one that is so vast and unfamiliar. It affects the way we view our place in this world and our scope of the complexity of the world around us.

Sometimes we encounter God in a similar manner. We can hear of this immeasurable, indescribable, Creator of the universe and be told He exists and loves us beyond what we could ever imagine. That's one way to know God. But...when He interjects Himself into our lives in a visible manner, it floors us. We are awestruck, absolutely amazed, that such a vast God could actually have a personal interest in us. There are God-moments that occur in our own lives when we can truly sense God at work, right beside us. These experiences are indescribable and fill us with a sensation of wonder.

God's in the close call you had where something out of the ordinary happened that saved you. God's in the eye-catching, spectacular sunset you see out of your car window on the highway heading home. God is in the voice of the doctor who calls with news of good test results. God is also there, working through the hands of the doctors who provide healing treatment. God is in the feeling you get when you help someone in need. God is in the peace you find in prayer. God is in the voice of a small child who looks up into your face, for no reason at all, and unexpectedly says, "I love you."

We may think we are far from God, but He's always out there, and he *will* show up in our lives. I guarantee it. I can't tell you when or where, but if you scan the horizons of your life, you'll see Him. God shows up unexpectedly. He takes us by surprise. He rises out of the deep to personally touch our lives, making himself undeniably visible through His works. When these moments occur, we stop our engines, and we run for our cameras, even if it's only to take a snapshot that remains indelibly impressed on our memories.

In the midst of the waves of life, keep watch. God is out there. He has risen, and He will surface again, perhaps right beside you, out of the deep and into your heart.

River of Freedom

*Eventually, all things merge into one, and a river runs through
it. The river was cut by the world's great flood and runs over
rocks from the basement of time. On some of the rocks are timeless
raindrops. Under the rocks are the words, and some of the words
are theirs. I am haunted by waters.*

~ Norman Maclean, "A River Runs Through It" ~

I am also haunted by waters: the waters of the river that bring
people into our lives and the waters that carry them away from
us. Some people view it as the river of life or the river of death. I
hope you can assuage any fear you might have of this river and
ask you to consider that all things do merge into one, and this
river that runs through it is a river of freedom.

They have become shadows of their former selves. The
transitions seemed to take place all at once, yet I know they
happened while I was busy living my life. The process of dying,

is quicker for some than it is for others, but for those who watch on as the lives of loved ones ebb and wane, it is often a grueling process. Within the span of perhaps a year, I watched all three of my maternal grandparents' children bow out of life. My once vital and creative mother has seriously declined in health and passed away, the result of five strokes and other maladies. My uncle, the man who was the tallest and most healthy character from my childhood, was moved to hospice, entered what had been phrased as "his last days," and went to God, his ashes being interred at the exact moment when his sister, my mother, passed. My aunt, the woman who could run circles around anyone when it came to mathematics and numbers, eventually suffered multiple strokes and diminishing health. These three individuals led full, wonderful lives, although age never really softens the blow of saying goodbye.

However, in the case of my close friend Whitney, the process was much different. At forty-seven years of age and the second oldest of four sisters, Whitney personifies the words spunky, strong-willed, and courageous. Having known her since she was fifteen years old, I have seen her set, attack, and complete goals one after another. I'm only scratching the surface when I mention that she has been on Outward Bound trips, attained her MSW, worked as a social worker, created magnificent sewing and quilting projects, and, I believe, continues to be an amazing wife and mother.

Having already battled triple negative breast cancer twice over six years, getting the news that it had returned for a third time with a vengeance was quite a blow. The decline in her health was relentless and horrific until she finally slipped back into the arms of God on February 18, 2011, and left her physical body. The process was painful to watch for everyone who loves her, but, through it all, Whitney displayed courage and grace.

I know there are many among us who have suffered a loss, and all of us have been left to cope with the aftermath of loss.

How do you respond? What can someone say to a loved one's parents, spouse, siblings, or children? I don't know if there are any right words. Sometimes, I think, just being there for support is the best one can do. I feel the need to embrace this topic a little more. Why do we fear and resist death? What happens to us when we make that mysterious and literally breathtaking journey?

The other day, while I was unpacking some books in my efforts to triage them for display, attic storage, or garage sale, I came across a paperback that Whitney gave me in 1996 when I was running programs for battered women's shelters, organizations that are close to her heart and by which she was once employed. The book is called *Getting Free: A Handbook for Women in Abusive Relationships*. I perused its pages, remembering the contents the way one recalls the lines on the face of a longtime friend. I remembered that, for many abused women, the fear of the unknown, the fear of what may happen after they leave the abusive relationship is often more frightening than the abuse itself because the abuse is, at least, predictable. This fear of the unknown is what prevents many women from taking that step toward safety and independence. It takes time and counseling for many women to see that "getting free" is, ultimately, the safest and most gratifying road to take, one that leads to a much better place.

After paging through the book, I began to realize that the process of dying is much like "getting free." We suffer in this hard life on Earth. In many ways, we feel abused by the trials we encounter during this life. Oh, for sure, it's punctuated by some incredible joys of family, friends, and accomplishments, but, ultimately, we're told, the joy we will all find in heaven will far surpass what we have experienced here on Earth. Pain and suffering will be a thing of the past. The problem is that many of us fear death because the bliss of heaven is a matter of faith. There are no lectures or workshops at local libraries from the multitudes of those who have crossed over to tell us, "C'mon. I did it, and so can you! Yes, I know it's scary, but the rewards are incredible." No, when it's our time to make the transition, each one of us must decide if we are going to pass from this life with grace and trust the word of God or be hindered with fear, clinging to this existence because life on Earth, with all its pain, as much as it regularly beats us down, is, at least, a known quantity.

While I gathered my thoughts for this writing, I went strolling along McCann Mill Road, a quiet, dirt road that parallels the Lamington River in Pottersville, NJ. It was the first day of a very warm spell we had where the snow and ice on the ground seemed incongruous with the warmth of the air. Like Jesus' parables, God continually teaches us through metaphor in our lives. So, I went looking for whatever it was that I was supposed to see for inspiration, and, before long, I found it. More accurately, I should say, it found me. As the river came into view, I was abruptly moved to stop. I like to think that Whitney led me to where I needed to be in order for her to show me what she wanted to communicate. There was suddenly no more wondering on my part. In an instant, I knew what I wanted to express. The message was completely formed in my head, and I could not get home fast enough to begin writing.

I was struck with the way the trees along the river's bank seemed to be clutching on to the earth for dear life, their roots resembling sinewy fingers straining to keep the mass of each tree from falling prey to the river's erosion. The overhanging trees seemed to fear the river because they knew that the waters carried away anything that fell into it. In the water underneath the spreading branches were hollow trunks of once majestic trees. There were also fragments of other trees' branches, swept up in the current, floating away from their parent trees and on to a new place where they could no longer be seen by the woods, eventually to return to the Earth from which they originated. As they floated by, one could almost hear the trees call out to their water-borne kin,

> Stop! Please! Come back! Where are you going? You're part of us, the land. Some of us created you, and some of us sustained you, and some of us sprouted from the seeds from your branches. We love you, and we need you to stay and make leaves with us and provide shade and comfort.

I imagined that the floating branches might have called back from their journey in reply,

> Dear, beloved trees and saplings, the time has come for you to manage without us. Our time in the woods has ended. We are being carried to a different place to be reunited with and absorbed by our Earth that sustains you. Be happy for us, for we are no longer clutching to existence. Instead, we now feel incredibly weightless, supported in this river we once feared. We will always love you and remember you, and we will see you again. Be strong, but when your time being trees is done, we will be waiting for you, in a wonderful place, a different place, where you will find your eternal roots.

The river itself was swollen with the runoff from the melting snow. The surging waters washed and eroded underneath and around shelves of snow and ice that once covered the surface and now hung precarious, cracked, stiff, and protruding from the snow-laden banks, not yet willing to relent to the warming temperatures. Listening closely to the babble, I began to hear the frozen, icy shelves call out to the melted snow in the waters,

Wait! Why are you leaving us? Why have you disappeared? We all fell to this land as snowflakes in the great storms, each one of us unique. We covered the earth in purest white. We survived the coldest, darkest nights and greeted the dawn with sparkling, silvery splendor. We are so sad to watch you go, and we feel like we are shrinking without you here, for you are our brothers and sisters.

But the melted snow chuckled and responded in return,

Silly snow, we haven't disappeared, only changed form. We've lost our frozen structure, but you and we will always share the same essence. Do not be sad for us, for we're not traveling too far away. We're just going home, home to the Bay and the Great Ocean. When your season is finished, you will also wash into the river and become one with the Bay, and then we will all be part of the same, Great Ocean again, an Ocean full of life and diversity, free to move in currents and no longer frozen in place. Some of us fell as snow after you, yet have melted before you, but we will watch for you when you, too, change form and come to us, and together we will be adorned with froth and more pure than any snow.

Similarly, our loved ones who are called back to God are beloved branches of a mighty family tree, but they have traveled back to the source that will continue to sustain us all. Each person, a snowflake so unique, has not disappeared— only changed form—and has flowed down that River of Freedom and into the Great Ocean of Heaven where they are waiting for us, where there is no more pain, where they are not frozen in place, where there is no more cancer or disease, where they wait for us adorned with freedom and are more pure than any snow could ever be. They have followed the river.

Interestingly, my aunt was never a very religious woman, and she was the one most reluctant to accept the journey out of this earthly realm. My mother, my uncle, and Whitney are all strong in their belief in their Creator. They all trust in God and, consequently, have all been more accepting and relaxed. Many of our loved ones knew and know that death is but a portal through which we must all pass, some sooner than others, but in a short time, we will all be united with each other in God's embrace.

I know some of you have had curious things happen to you since a loved one has passed. They may not be lectures or workshops led by the "dearly departed," but there are nudges from beyond, things that let you know your loved one was safe and with God. On the morning of February 19, just twelve hours after Whitney made her journey to freedom, I had a dream. I saw Whitney at the ocean's edge on a broad, sandy beach. She was surrounded by ten people, but the image did not linger long before I woke. I assumed it was just a snapshot out of my memory, a scene of when Whitney was trying to get a stinging jellyfish out of her bathing suit when a bunch of us were visiting Fripp Island, SC, many years ago. The next night, I had the exact same dream, only this time it was longer and more detailed. Whitney was on the same beach, in the same scene and surrounded by the same group, but this time I could see that she was encircled by ten family members who had already journeyed down the river. All of her grandparents, two of her uncles, her great grandmother, and others were there hugging her. More people were walking up the beach to greet her, coming from a long staircase that led up a steep dune at the head of the beach.

I was only a spectator, sitting on the sand some thirty feet away from the group who seemed to be unaware of my presence.

But then, I was surprised by Whitney's maternal grandmother who turned, looked right into my eyes, and smiled, before returning her attention to greeting Whitney who had her back to me and her arms up in the air. The group was consumed in celebration, and then Whitney glanced over her left shoulder, looked at me with a big smile, and said, "Hey, Gord." At that point, the image faded, and I woke wrapped in peace because this time I knew it wasn't a memory. This was a gift from God. Whitney came back a second night to make certain I knew this, and I believe she wants us to know she's happy and surrounded by love—and so are *all* of our loved ones who have passed out of this physical existence.

So, what can one say to those of us remaining on the banks of this river? Maybe just this… Think of your loved ones, and they will be with you. Hold them close to your soul, and they will embrace you, for in many ways, all of our loved ones who have gone to God are now more alive than when they were living their physical lives. Although they have now joined the others who have been swept up in the divine river's current of transformation, I know they still love us, they are happy, and they want us to be happy for them because they are now enveloped in a Peace and a Love so alive and so much greater than anyone could ever find in this world. The journey holds absolutely nothing to fear.

To those who have made the journey, we know you didn't want to leave us, but we also know that, when your time came, you did not hesitate to make that leap into the realm defined so clearly by your personal faith. And when our times and purposes for being part of this life's tree and seasons are finished, you will be there with God waiting to greet us in a place where all of us will be reunited. In 2 Corinthians 3:17 it says, "Now the Lord is the Spirit, and where the Spirit of the Lord is, there is freedom." To Whitney and everyone else on our minds who have left this earth, we love you. We thank God that our paths crossed in this life, but they will again when we journey to God's Kingdom, a journey on a river of freedom for which no handbook is needed for getting free.

Moving at the Speed of God

Walking to church the other day, I watched as a cyclist swerved into the road, completely unaware that there was a car behind him and about to turn into the church's parking lot. The car swerved, averting the collision, but it startled the cyclist. However, the unexpected result of this event was the response of the cyclist. Upon noticing his error, the cyclist began shouting at the driver of the car! Beginning with a salutation unfit for print, the man addressed the driver at the top of his lungs, "Hey, slow down! Where are you going in such a hurry? Maybe that'll give you something to pray about this morning!"

Indeed, I thought, perhaps the driver should pray for you, Mr. Cyclist! What is it about human nature that often finds a way to blame others for our own mistakes? The cyclist completely missed the point. Due to the driver's quick reactions, he got to keep riding his bike instead of paying a visit to the hospital. Maybe he was embarrassed for having swerved, or maybe his outburst was just a knee-jerk reaction. The whole event, after all, took place in a matter of seconds, in the blink of an eye—at the speed of God.

At the speed of God? How fast might that be? Can it be quantified? Is it faster than the speed of light, 186,000 miles per second (696,600,000 mph)? No, I don't think it has anything to do with the physical laws of nature. The speed of God, I think, moves within our hearts. God's creation is ever-present and never-ending. God's plan for us was begun long before we drew our first breaths and will continue long after we leave our earthly bodies.

John Muir once wrote,

The grand show is eternal. It is always sunrise somewhere; the dew is never dried all at once; a shower is forever falling; vapor is ever rising. Eternal sunrise, eternal dawn and gloaming, on sea and continents and islands, each in its turn, as the round earth rolls.

Our lives? They're all part of God's eternal show, and I believe we need to learn from them. Every twist and turn along the way of life holds kernels of epiphany, seeds of sudden realization strewn about at our feet, and all we have to do is be aware of the opportunities for divine enrichment.

How fast is the speed of God? It can seem as slow as the turning leaf or as fast as the starlight hurdling through the heavens. God shows us every day the path to enlightenment, but often we get so caught up in our humanity that we fail to see or recognize the way. We fool ourselves into thinking that someone, often someone other than ourselves, is to blame for everything, when, in reality, it is all part of God's plan and in God's hands.

It's a hard thing for humans to do, to respond with love. Pierre Teilhard de Chardin, the visionary French Jesuit, paleontologist, biologist, and philosopher once said,

Someday, after mastering the winds, the waves, the tides, and gravity, we shall harness for God the energies of love, and then, for a second time in the history of the world, man will have discovered fire.

God, you see, wants us to respond with love and let it burn in our hearts. My wish for that cyclist is that he might look back and appreciate the way in which God spared him on that Sunday morning, and may he ponder how his days on Earth could have ended very suddenly. What will he do with the rest of his time, the rest of his life? Maybe that question will give *him* something to pray about this morning. Maybe he will have an epiphany at the speed of God, and maybe, if he's lucky, he will discover fire.

Maximized Abilities

I've decided most of us are lazier than we think we are and complain far too much. Does that make you uncomfortable? Good! It unnerves me, too, but maybe we need to feel that way in order for us to realize our true potential. Our gifts and abilities are often our biggest hindrances.

The hamlet of Pottersville, NJ, sits in a valley, surrounded on three sides by large hills. The only moderate terrain follows the Lamington River southward out of town. All of the five, major roads leading into Pottersville are beautiful, popular routes for cyclists, as two follow the river, and the other three offer spectacular views of the surrounding, hay-roll crested hills and fields.

I jumped into my car one morning and encountered a bicycle tour that was just beginning to stream down Pottersville Road from the east. As I headed up the road, I realized the tour was comprised of hundreds of riders. Most of the cyclists I saw were enjoying the cruise down the 1.3-mile descent, having already conquered the .6-mile climb from Route 206. "These bikers are enjoying the payoff," I thought. They were riding two or three abreast and sporting smiles on many of their faces. The climb they had just completed is challenging, but it's nowhere near as challenging as it would have been if their direction were reversed. The winding hill climb out of Pottersville is a killer, as the 1.3-mile incline makes it seem like twice that distance.

I was traveling slowly in my car, being cautious of the continuous stream of riders coming down in the opposite direction. About two thirds of the way up the hill, I spotted another rider going my direction—up the hill. This guy, obviously not with the tour, was tackling the extra challenging side, but he was showing fatigue and moving slower than most riders I've seen in his position. The stream of celebratory riders was still cascading down the other side of the hill, and I was slowing down considerably because I had to pass between the mass of coasting cyclists on my left and the solitary climber on my right.

Then I saw it. The rider going up the hill didn't have a left leg. I'm not implying that he had a prosthetic limb. I mean he had no limb at all beneath his left knee! Amazing questions raced through my head. How difficult must it be for this guy to get on his bike? How hard is it for him to dismount? Plus, (and I don't care about how many gears he may have) how much harder than others must it be for this rider to keep up his momentum and crank *UP* the Pottersville hill? His right leg was doing the work of two! Most recreational cyclists rest their legs on the upstroke. This guy was using his right leg, foot, cycling shoe, and pedal to put as much energy and effort into his upstroke as he was into his downstroke. His spinning was labored, for sure, but for good reason, and I was deeply touched by the courage, strength, and determination displayed by this rider.

That solitary cyclist has humbled me. He was an unexpected wake-up call. I wondered if the other riders noticed him as they hurtled down the hill, smugly celebrating the reward for their climb, which was less than half that of this solitary climber. Who was handicapped the most? It wasn't the one-legged cyclist. I decided it was the riders in the tour, the ones who get to draft behind each other, the ones who get to have police stop traffic for them at major intersections, the ones who ride with support vehicles. As much as they worked hard to reach their common goal, their handicap resided in the assistance they received along the journey. I'm sure they appreciated the vistas and cool breezes on their necks after a hard climb, but nowhere near as much as this one-legged rider who had no assistance at all.

This applies to all of us…all of us with God-given talents and abilities. Do we maximize our abilities, or do we take the easier route and let complacency seep into our lives? Do we appreciate the gifts, grace, and the abundant, simple pleasures in life that surround us, or do we find ourselves blindly wanting more and more? Do we challenge ourselves to do more than most would expect? Do we realize how much more we could accomplish if we doubled our efforts, and do we recognize the gift we have in that choice? Do we see the hidden blessing in voluntarily trying harder because we wanted to do so instead of being forced to do it?

We mustn't allow our abilities and our abundant gifts from God to handicap us, so I've decided today to reinvent my own ride, my ride through life, and I'm going to approach it with the mindset of that one-legged rider. You're invited! Come and join me on the tour.

Fix Me

During the Civil War, wounded soldiers often knew death was approaching by the extent and nature of their wounds. Field surgeons, nurses, and attendants did what they could to extend life or make their patients comfortable, but, often, even the best efforts were to no avail. Knowing rigor mortis would set in on the heels of their last breath, soldiers often laid themselves out, legs straight, and hands folded across the stomach. The wounded men who were not able to move often relied on others to assist in this morbid task. In a weakened plea for aid, they would look toward the medical staff for help. "Fix me," they'd say, "Fix me right." Legs extended, a soldier's socks would be pinned together at the toes, and his hands would be secured, folded on the abdomen, and he would find solace in knowing he was prepared to receive death's kiss and journey to God.

It's sad, isn't it, this scene of death? Yet it happened countless times to countless soldiers, many of whose names are now lost in the tides of time. It's a tragic snapshot of nineteenth century warfare, taken from a page in the history books, and no longer encroaches on our current view of the world. Or does it?

Consider Dan. Dan had the good life, the one many people term successful. He came from a family with all the right connections. He was an Ivy League graduate, and, upon receiving his advanced degree, he landed a position in an extremely respected brokerage company. Dan married the love of his life, a girl he had known since high school. Together, they bought a large home in suburban Connecticut and had two, beautiful children. Dan had wealth and power and security. He was the captain of his ship. Life was idyllic...idyllic until the day he answered the phone call that shattered his world. The tractor-trailer, moving at too high a rate of speed and carrying a full load, tipped on a curve. The convertible didn't stand a chance, and Dan's wife and two children were gone in seconds.

To ease the pain, devastation, and emptiness, Dan turned to alcohol. What started as a couple of drinks per night soon turned into more drinks than he could remember. His business performance failed, and when it seemed like it could get no worse, his position was terminated, and, subsequently, he lost his home. Dan started to drown in depression, uncertainty, and loneliness. He was broken beyond self-repair, or so it seemed. The one constant in his life was the church that Dan had attended as a boy. Granted, he hadn't graced its doorway in years, but he remembered that whenever he returned to his boyhood home and did attend, he was greeted by warm smiles and a sense of comfort and familiarity he felt nowhere else.

That Sunday, when things seemed so far out of his control, Dan went back to that church. He slipped into his favorite pew, third from the back, and he listened. He listened to the words of hope. He mouthed the lyrics to the hymns of peace. And he tried to imagine the type of love the minister said was available to anyone. "Anyone? Even me?" thought Dan. Somewhere in the midst of the sermon, tears filled Dan's eyes, and he gave up. He gave up trying to do it all by himself. He gave up thinking he was untouchable. He gave up trying to gauge the success of his life by what he had or lost. He gave up trying to run away from this love of God that he had always heard about but never embraced. "Fix me," he prayed. "Oh, God, please, I can't do it by myself anymore. I don't know what to do...or where to look...or what to say. My life is in pieces, and I just need you. Please...fix me!"

Sound familiar? It happens to more people than we know, yet not everyone relinquishes control to God. Some people struggle, caught in emotional quicksand, unable to escape. The lucky ones stop struggling and hold on to God.

Are you looking for a more experiential example? Last year, a man walked into my church very early on a Sunday morning. I was setting up the microphones and checking the sound when I heard the front door unlatch and open. A man in his early 20s stepped into the narthex looking bedraggled. I walked through the swinging doors and met him.

"Good morning," I greeted.

"Is it alright if I pray?" he asked in a light, Irish accent.

"Of course. Go on in," I said.

He went to the front, right pew and sat down. I busied myself with the soundboard and sorting bulletins, not wanting to disturb our visitor. He had begun by sitting upright in the pew, but after five minutes, he was slumped over the pew wall, hands folded in front of him. I could see his body heaving with quiet sobs. After another five minutes, he gathered himself and walked out of the sanctuary. I smiled at him as he approached the exterior door of the narthex.

"I prayed to God and asked Him for an answer," he said. "He spoke to me, and He gave me one."

This visitor gave himself up to God. Much like one of those Civil War soldiers, he basically said, "I can't do this anymore. I'm ready for you to take the wheel. Fix me. Fix me right." God heard him, and my visitor found his direction. It happened right here, folks, right in the front pew in New Vernon, NJ. In the church where I work and worship! In one of God's churches, right before my eyes! This exchange, this dialogue, isn't something that only happens in exotic situations. It's not something that only occurs to special, "chosen" people up on a holy mountain top. It happens to people of every socio-economic strata and every race and in any hometown you can imagine.

But not everyone is as open to it as others. Sometimes comfort can obscure the view, and it is, at times, more difficult for people of means to have this dialogue experience with God. Who makes up the group "people of means?" Well, a good deal of us, certainly. According to one source I found, the average world per capita income in 2010 was about $8,000 per year, but the majority of people scrape by with a meager $2,000 or less per year income. So, why is it often more difficult for people of means to have this dialogue experience with God? Because comfort and wealth can create a false impression of independence. Because a comfortable lifestyle can create the illusion that everything is under the person's control. I'll quote from the publication *Culture, International*.

> Poor people, sick people, desperate people will, by and large, be among the most religious for a very good reason: Those on the ragged edge have the most acute sense of the fragility of life, of their own contingency. Wealthy, educated folk have a much more profound sense of being "in control." What do they need with a heavenly father or benign providential care or direction? They have an AMEX black card.

But as important as our positions at work might happen to be, as large as our salaries or bank accounts are, as impressive as our real estate holdings or stock portfolios may be, we all walk a tightrope, and our possessions are no more protective than the blue sky over our heads or the void beneath our feet on the wire.

Ancient people believed that the day's blue sky and the nighttime's starlit firmament was a solid dome that covered the Earth and was attached to the edges of it, that the stars were attached to this dome, and that heaven lay just beyond the dome. How would that belief affect you? Would you feel more secure? Imagine how that belief might alter one's perception of security. Imagine how people must have felt when they first learned that the sky was not a solid, protective shield, and that there was a seemingly endless space and universe just above their heads, over which they had no detailed knowledge or control. I think it must have been a frightening realization!

When security is stripped away, people often turn to God. The down-and-out, the ill, the poor, the lonely, the people that have hit rock bottom often are the ones who turn to God and other people more regularly for help and support. Just like those Civil War soldiers, they look toward others for assistance, guidance, and salvation, to help them do what they are no longer able to do on their own. They understand, in a very intimate manner, that they are part of something much more vast than themselves that they do not control. They see God as their net beneath the high wire.

Do you remember a point in your life when you thought you were invincible? Perhaps you took a joy ride in someone else's car, or you started smoking cigarettes, or you drove a car while you were drinking? "Nothing's going to happen to me," you thought. Then there's the moment when you wake up to reality, when the sands of life shift under your feet. A friend has a serious automobile accident, someone you know or love gets lung cancer or some other life-threatening illness, or there's an arrest for a DUI. Your sense of independence and superiority, as a result, is severely challenged.

When I was a freshman in college, one of my friends, a talented musician who played piano and used to jam with me, was finishing his senior year at my former high school. He got the lead in the school's spring musical. His performance as Harold Hill in *The Music Man* was phenomenal. During the cast party, he left his friends and fellow cast members saying he needed to get cigarettes in town. He never returned. His body was found early the following morning in his car, which was parked between two maintenance trucks in the high school parking lot. On that starlit night in May, Séan ran a hose from his exhaust pipe in through his driver's window and slowly fell asleep, never to open his eyes again. No one saw it coming.

Just two months after Séan's funeral, another friend of mine was completing summer school classes after her sophomore year at the University of Maine in Orono. She was riding her bike home from the university library one night in late July and was hit by a motorcycle. My friend wasn't wearing a helmet, and her head was crushed by the impact. I was a pall bearer at her funeral. On one of my trips carrying flowers to the hearse, I entered the viewing room at the moment the casket lid was being closed. I realized I was the last person on Earth who would ever see Eileen.

Now, there's nothing unique about these experiences. Unfortunately, we've all had them, or will have something similar to them. But here's the thing…while sad, these experiences opened my eyes to the fact that things will not go as planned, and there will be many times when I know I will have no control and will just need to let God take the wheel. There have been, are, and always will be surprises—happy and sad—and, hopefully, they point us in a direction that makes us more mindful of the fact that we need to trust God with our lives, mindful of how helpless and vulnerable we really are.

Sometimes we don't like the endings of life's stories...
but sometimes we do. Remember Dan and his decision to
acknowledge that God is in control? That morning at worship
in the church of his childhood, when he asked God to fix him, a
sense of peace enveloped Dan, and he felt the presence of God
embracing him. Several years later, Dan found himself in a new
home. He never stopped loving the family he lost, but he had
fallen in love again and remarried. His abuse of alcohol was a
thing of the past, he had been offered a new financial position
with a smaller, private company, and he and his new wife
contemplated having children.

I'm going to let you in on a secret. One of the things that frustrate
clergy is their message's lack of longevity. Occasionally, people
will come back to preachers saying how they contemplated
the sermon or describe how the message affected their lives.
More often, though, the topic has been forgotten by Sunday
lunch. It has less to do with the preacher than it does with the
encroachment of life's demands on our attention. So, in light of
this, I'd like to issue you a challenge, and it's one with which I
often challenge myself.

At some point during the next seven days, in the midst of the
overabundant blessings of our day-to day lives, carve out a time
to think about your weak point, your fear, or a part of your life
that just isn't working or that seems out of control. After you do
that, ask God for help in a deliberate manner. Acknowledge that
God is in control. Admit that God is your safety net. Trust that
God cares for YOU and will help YOU. Open yourself. Fully
reveal your emotions and your heart. Don't hold back! Tear
down the walls you may have erected between you and God.
Turn your particular concern over to your heavenly father, and
see what happens.

Now, this might feel unusual because some people,
especially us independent, wall-building types like me, have to
become accustomed to asking for help. We like to do things on

our own and in our own way, but we all need help, and we all need forgiveness, *and we all need grace, especially from God.* But, sometimes, we need to stop our struggling and ask for God's help.

I remember one particular time I went fishing with my son Cory and my wife Veronica. We always release our fish. Well, on this occasion Veronica caught a bass, the first fish she had ever caught. When landed, this fish struggled and flipped and flopped and flopped and flipped and struggled, constantly using its own efforts to free itself from its predicament. All the while, Veronica was trying to remove the hook saying, "Calm down. Shhhh. Relax. Relax. I'll get you out of this mess. I know, it hurts when the hook goes back through. I know." Eventually, the bass calmed down enough to allow Veronica to slide the hook back out of its mouth and release him back into the water, its problem resolved. "There ya go," she said.

We can learn from that bass and its experience. I want you to imagine that you are the fish, and you're caught in some predicament and don't know what to do, and God is saying Veronica's words to you while he's trying to free you. You see, sometimes, we can't unhook ourselves from our problems. It's at these times that we need to stop our struggling and let God help us. It's really very simple to begin. All we have to do is pray and talk to our Father in heaven in very simple words and language, "God...please...fix me! Fix me right."

Pray it with me.

"God...please...fix me! Fix me right."

Amen.

The Point of Departure

There are two ski jump towers in Lake Placid. I don't know if you've ever seen them, but, looking at them from the road directly across from the Olympic Jumping Complex, these huge, incongruous monoliths of steel and concrete rise abruptly out of the forested landscape, reaching heights of 90 and 120 meters. Not long ago, my family and I were vacationing in the Adirondacks, and I was looking at these towers and metaphorically thinking how the relationship between a ski jumper and the tower is a lot like the one between parent and child and how, for those of us who have lost a parent, it can help teach us about the resulting void as well.

Imagine yourself as an athlete entering the bottom of the tower, and, stepping into an elevator, you're enveloped by this structure that raises you up to the top, and as you ride the glass-walled elevator upwards, you can look out at the expanding views of the surrounding countryside. Now, for some people, this ride might be a little frightening because you're raised way up off the ground in what is essentially a steel and glass box, but with that fear also comes the excitement of looking out at the gorgeous river and mountains. This is very similar to what happens to us during childhood, isn't it? Our mothers and our fathers raise us up; they show us the world and our place in the world from a very personal and unique perspective. There are times that are frightening, and there are times that are just so incredibly amazing, but, all the time, you're being prepared for departure. Ultimately, the goal of any ski jumper or child is independence.

When you get to the top of the elevator, the steel doors open, and you walk out onto a glass-walled observation deck on top of the tower. You've made a transition, and you're sort of on your own, but not really. True, you're not enveloped by that structure anymore, but you still feel safe and protected. This is similar to the time we spend in high school. You step out on your own a little bit more, but, still, your parents are right there for you.

Suddenly, as you round the corner, you get your first look down the jump. It's the path you realize you are about to take, and you get to that moment when you have to sit on a bench, slide yourself out to the middle, and put your skis in two tracks of ice. You feel a growing rush of adrenaline and fear. This is synonymous with graduating from high school or college. Everything you've been raised to be has brought you to this moment. Given the signal, you push off from the home bench and you're on your own, your speed increasing as you get further down the icy tracks.

At this point, the adrenaline rush is tempered by reassurance. As a young person leaving home, you know that, even though you're no longer enveloped by your parents, they are there. Your mother or father is right there for you. You know that you're in contact with them because you can feel their support. In life, if you need anything at all, you can go right back to your mother's or father's support. You can go right back to either of your parents, and they will be there for you. They support you emotionally, and sometimes financially, whenever it's needed. In ski jumping, you need this vital, supportive contact directly underneath you in order to push off at the edge and begin your solo flight.

Solo flight… Smack in the middle of this comparison, I caught myself looking at these jumps and thinking, "and then there's that moment in time and place where that ski jump ends, the point of departure…and there's a huge drop." I've been there. Anyone who has lost a parent has been at this place. Suddenly, mom or dad is not there anymore physically to support you. But if you're a ski jumper, you have the comfort of knowing that after you go off the end of that jump, the ground comes up to meet you again. It is never, during the remainder of your entire jump, any more than seven to ten feet away from you.

You don't really see this when you watch ski jumping on television. It appears as if the jumper is soaring high above mother earth, but, in reality, the ground is never far below the athlete. As a jumper, you're flying in space, and you're on your own. You're fixed on your landing point. You don't see the ground directly underneath you, but you're confident that the ground is there, somewhere. You can't touch it while you're in flight, but there's a reassuring knowledge that the ground is right there, never far from you during your flight. You sail through the air with grace, and you prepare for the landing, for you know that every jumper's flight will come to an end, and you will touch the earth once more.

For those of us who have endured the passing of a parent, hold your form; fly with grace for as long as you can. We are in the flight of our lives, but, similar to the ski jumper, find comfort in the certainty that your mother or father is never far away from you. You may not feel them, and you may not see them, but they are there. Most assuredly, they are there watching you fly, as proud of you as they have ever been. Eventually, you will meet again. You will touch down and be joined together as surely as the ski jumper will be reunited with the earth, but your reunion will be more comforting, warmer, and even sweeter.

Gifting Divinity

"What we are is God's gift to us. What we become is our gift to God."

~ Eleanor Powell ~

Her face was bright, but her eyes revealed a darkness that refused to be illuminated by the light of day. It was apparent that she had seen more than her share of pain, more than her share of want. At eleven years of age, her eyes looked like those of an adult, someone who had experienced life far beyond her tender years.

Known simply as Tee, this young girl stood next to our boxes of toys and clothes that the youth group had brought to the mountain hollers of eastern Kentucky on our mission trip, and now it was her turn to choose some items to bring home with her. She did not look up very often, unfamiliar and a bit uncomfortable with the luxury of choosing a few stuffed animals and selecting some items to wear. Tee's roots were in poverty, and as she stood still in her yellow fleece, gazing at the abundance before her, her eyes fell upon an eighteen-inch-tall, stuffed penguin.

"I love penguins!" Tee exclaimed in her southern drawl.

"Well then, it should go home with you," one of our members responded.

"Really?"

"It's yours. Go ahead. Take it with you."

I don't know if you have ever felt as if God was standing beside you, but I could feel something at work, something beyond the people gathered at the Cordia School in Lotts Creek, Kentucky. Although it was beginning to snow from the mottled, grey sky above our heads, there was warmth that embraced us, and at that moment, deep in Tee's eyes a spark ignited, a sparkle shimmered, and this girl began to raise her eyes. She made eye contact with all of us, and she began to talk about herself, about her family, and a little about her life. As we traded comments and revelations, we heard not the voice of a child but one that would be expected to come from a young woman. Tee had become comfortable speaking with us. She was confident. Her shyness and reticence had melted away to reveal an adorable personality.

After a few minutes, Tee began to search through the boxes at her feet and was encouraged to take what she liked, and, eventually, she did. Gathering items in her arms, it was apparent that this girl was immersed in the moment, gathering joy along with material possessions. She was truly thankful, so very deeply appreciative for the experience.

When she was finished, we expected Tee to retire to her mother's car and depart in the manner of the other children who were invited to the school that morning, but she didn't. Instead, someone from the school staff mentioned Tee's ability to sing, so, upon looking up, with her arms and eyes filled with joy, Tee broke into song after some encouragement. We all stood transfixed, hearing a voice of confidence, a sweet, melodic tone that we were surprised to hear coming from the mouth of a child. Her voice sung of loss, sung of remembrance, sung of pride and honor, and the soul behind the voice complemented the lyrics. It was apparent that this girl knew of these things and emotions through experience, and as Tee spun through the verses and choruses, we heard the voice of an angel signing to us.

Suddenly, I think we all realized that the greater gift received that day was the one God gave to us all through this young girl. We were gifted the presence and peace of divinity. We felt it inside us, and as we embraced Tee after her song, as we said good-bye, the spirit of God embraced us all. And in the silence that followed, there in that austere, Kentucky holler, while the snow fell upon our heads, the grace of God alighted on our hearts.

Useless!…Useful!

In the dark, early morning hours of April 26, 1865, a Federal cavalry detail descended on Richard H. Garrett's farm, just south of Port Royal, Virginia, searching for Abraham Lincoln's assassin. The Union troopers had actually been led to the area by a false report of a sighting that, coincidentally, had put them right on the trail of John Wilkes Booth and David Herold. Information provided by locals sent them to the Garrett farm… where Garrett's son Jack volunteered the information that both Booth and Herold were sleeping in the barn.

The troopers surrounded the barn and told the two fugitives to surrender. Herold did, hysterically protesting that he was innocent; the soldiers told him to shut up and tied him to a tree. Booth, in contrast, was defiant, theatrical to the last. When one of the troopers set fire to the barn, Booth got up and limped to the barn door, only to be shot through the neck by a revolver wielded by Union sergeant Boston Corbett. He claimed he had shot Booth because it appeared the fugitive was getting ready to shoot it out with the cavalrymen. Whatever the case, the bullet had severed Booth's spine. Booth lived until about 7:00 that morning, when he asked that his paralyzed arms be lifted so that he could look at his hands. "Useless! Useless!" he muttered a few times and then faded away.

Useless! Useless! How many of us reach points in our lives when we feel our efforts are useless…or that even we, ourselves, are useless? I know all of us, at some point in our lives, have dealt with pain and severe challenges: the loss of a spouse, child, or close relative or friend, unemployment, the news of inoperable cancer, endless abuse with no clear way out, drug or alcohol addiction.

When those things happen, it's often very hard to climb out of that pit in which we find ourselves. The depression can become so overpowering that we stop caring about others. We think no one loves us. We lose our link with friends, family, and community. We even stop loving and caring about ourselves. The depression can become a kind of emotional paralysis. Useless! For those of us who have not been down that road, it is hard to understand how people's emotions can sink that low.

Put your hands up in front of you and look at them. Keep them up. Imagine looking at those hands and feeling like they are completely useless. I pray it's impossible for you to do, but it happens, and, when it does, it can be devastating. Okay, hands down.

I had a friend who took his own life not too long ago after battling extreme emotional disorders. He felt as if he had no hope left and nowhere to turn. He had lost his marriage and his relationships with his children. He had seen his career slip through his fingers, and his house was in foreclosure. The last time I saw him alive was when I visited him in the hospital after his last unsuccessful attempt, and, with tears running down his cheeks, he held up his hands and said to me, "I can't believe my hands betray me like they do." I knew what he meant. His hands had tried to take his life eight times. His hands had threatened the lives of his wife and his two, young daughters. His hands had killed two family pets. "It happens when I go off my meds," he continued, "but that's not even the worst part. The worst happens when I'm *ON* my meds, and I realize I feel nothing when I'm taking them. I have looked at my daughter sitting in a chair and have had no more feeling for her than I do for the chair." Looking at his hands, he choked up and finished with, "I'm useless. I can't do anything anymore."

Think about that statement, "I...can't...do...anything... anymore." Jesus tells us that we should come to Him with all our troubles, that He will bear us up. But I wonder how many of us really believe that or practice that. Who is this God that would be so interested in my problems? There are much larger problems in the world. What difference could my problems make to Him? Why would He have time for me?

It still happens occasionally, but when daughter Melina and son Cory were younger, some of my most precious moments were when my children had a problem or a boo-boo and they would look up to me for help, sometimes with tears in their eyes. "Daddeee!" they'd cry, and it would melt my heart. Have you ever had one of those moments? You're a parent or an aunt or uncle, godparent, whatever you might be, and the special children in your life come up to you..."mommy!"..."daddy!" You may fix the problem and console them with your love and compassion, but the heart-melting part is caused by their coming to you in the first place coupled with the joy you feel when you get to make your love a tangible part of their lives.

So, I'm hoping we can make it a habit of doing the same with God as our father. When we have these bigger-than-life problems—or any problem for that matter—why don't we go running full speed into the arms of God and say, *"Daddy, I'm hurting so badly. I don't know what to do. Please make me feel better."*?

God is our father, and what parent wouldn't want his child to go to him when they're hurting? Ask for help from God. When you have that adult-sized boo-boo, run to Him for help. Let Him wrap His arms around you. Feel His love surround you. You are never alone. Nothing makes God happier than His children coming to him.

Jesus said, "Let the little children come to me; do not stop them; for it is to such as these that the kingdom of God belongs." Guess what, you guys? He's talking about us! We are all God's children. We should all go to him because the kingdom of God that we all talk about belongs to all of us! And that love He promises is given freely to all of us!

In 1978, a band called Kansas had a huge hit with the release of a song called "Dust in the Wind," which, by the way, was recorded in the town where I work, New Vernon, NJ. I'm sure many of you know the lyrics.

"Dust in the wind...
All we are is dust in the wind.
Dust in the wind...
All we are is dust in the wind."

There was even a mournful violin solo that accompanied it. Whoa! How depressing is that? Well, maybe not for Kansas. They sold a lot of records with that song. But here's the thing; when it was released, everybody was singing it. I worry because at some level, when something is repeated over and over, I fear that people start to believe it. So, I've got to tell you; don't believe it. The song's message is just plain wrong.

As the French philosopher and Jesuit priest Pierre Teilhard de Chardin once said, "We are not human beings having a spiritual experience; we are spiritual beings having a human experience." We are *spiritual beings* having a *human experience.* Our spiritual life is eternal. This earthly life—every part of it—is temporary. Yes, joy comes to all of us, but that doesn't negate the fact that the lives we lead here are hard. It's not a matter of *if* we will experience pain; it's *when* and *how often.* We'll get our guts ripped out in this world; it's just the way it is. We will get emotionally eviscerated. Loss of love, failure of a marriage, loss of a job, whatever it might be, it's going to hurt, and it's going to hurt real badly, *BUT* we can get through it. How does that happen? By turning to God as our father and having a true link to a supportive community. We are called to serve and minister to others. God often works through us to show His love and caring. Through our service to our fellow sisters and brothers on this earth, we act as the agents of God in this human experience, and we restore ourselves as well.

I was once running with my dog, Aztec, on a gravel road in Pottersville. Now, Aztec is the kind of dog that doesn't always make the best decisions for himself, but he's a devoted, wonderful companion. Our deal is he keeps me company when I'm running, and I let him swim in the river at the midpoint of our run. Well, we were heading up the road, and a motorcycle came up slowly from behind us. Just as it was passing us, the rider revved his engine. Aztec got spooked by the sudden, loud sound and ran into me.

Did you ever watch those NFL films and see one of those frightening tackles where the receiver makes a mid-air catch, and his defender knocks the legs right out from underneath him. Yeah...that would be me. Aztec took me out in mid-stride, and it was all I could do to hold on to the leash as I skidded across the gravel. As if being knocked to the ground and sucking dust wasn't injury enough, insult was added when I caught a glimpse of the motorcyclist heading away from me...waving.

Getting up and brushing myself off, I saw that I had some cuts on my arm, hip, and hand, so when we got home from the run, the parts of my body that weren't hurt cared for the parts that were. Wounds were washed by my uninjured hand. Stones were picked from cuts by healthy fingers. Band-Aids were applied—and that made all of me feel better.

It's the same with community. When one or more members of the body of mankind are hurting, other members come to their aid. That's the way it's supposed to work. It's unnatural to act otherwise. Can you imagine never taking care of your aches, pains, and wounds? Of course not! *You*, whatever your training, whatever your experience or education, *you* always have a role to play in God's plan. *You* are needed. *You* are worthwhile. *You* are loved by God and others, and *you* are never ever useless!

Are we dust in the wind? No! Peter says,

> You are a chosen race, a royal priesthood, a holy nation, God's own people, in order that you may proclaim the mighty acts of Him who called you out of darkness into His marvelous light. Once you were not a people, but now you are God's people; once you had not received mercy, but now you have received mercy.

Friends, this same, divine mercy is meant to shine into the world through you and all people through our service for each other, and any pain that life dishes out on others can be mitigated by you. And any pain you may be feeling can be alleviated by your friends, your family, and your community.

Often in worship services, congregation members share the hand of fellowship with each other. Remember, sharing the hand of fellowship works even better when you leave the sanctuary! My friend who chose suicide didn't realize or receive this, so I want to make sure you understand this.

Okay… hold your hands up once again… right in front of your face. Stare and them and say out loud. "I am never alone. The light of God shines through me, through my *service* to others, and through others' *service* to me. I am *useful*! *Useful*!"

The String Bean Lesson

There she was at the kitchen sink, working on the cutting board. My mother was a very good cook, but she was even more frugal. She made it her business to see that nothing went to waste, even if she couldn't think of a use for it right away. Frugality was not only reserved for food products, it carried over to fabric swatches, old clothes, broken gadgets, and even people. Nobody sat idle for very long in our home without mom reminding us that there was weeding to be done, a dog to be brushed, or some other task to be accomplished.

Oftentimes, however, my mother would be completely content to let me watch her prepare meals in the kitchen. I recollect one day watching her prepare string beans. Now for those of you who think this means fetching a plastic bag of beans from a freezer, tearing open the bag, and dumping the contents into a pot of boiling water, you're far off the mark.

Her process began with a trip to Mrs. Cox's farm stand that used to be in Basking Ridge, NJ, on the southern side of Madisonville Road between the traffic light and the pond. My mother and our neighbor would pile us kids into the Dodge Coronet station wagon and drive several miles to get vegetables. When we got home, it was time to clean them. Clean them? Well, of course. They were fresh from the garden, so they still had dirt on them. After we washed the beans, we removed the stem tip from each bean and pulled the fibrous string from the crease along the length of the fruit. (Yes, string beans are fruit, since they are produced from flowers.) If the beans were extra-long, we might snap them in half to make them more bite sized.

When the process was completed, we had two piles; one contained the prepared beans, and the other contained the waste...err...I mean...non-edible parts. There was no waste in my mother's eyes. Quick as a rabbit and before anyone could imagine dumping the strings and stem tips into the trash, my mother would say, "off to the compost with those."

On one occasion, we were having company for dinner and had prepared a ponderous pile of string beans, enough beans for nine people. This time, when the moment came to dispose of the non-edible pile, my mother hesitated. She gave the pile a second look. "Wait a second, honey. Look through that pile again; there might be something good in there." Spreading the bits of bean stems out on a towel, I found she was right. There among the refuse were three whole beans. "Good thing we didn't throw those in the compost," she said with a wink. "As long as there's possibility and hope, it's always worth a second look. You never know what goodness you may find. You know what I mean?"

I knew what she meant. My mother was talking about more than string beans. She was talking about life. She was talking about how we treat other people, and she was referring to the way in which we treat ourselves. Her words had a spiritual, almost Biblical quality to them. How many times do we give up on something when the possibility of goodness still exists? Obviously, we shouldn't keep returning to situations that are toxic or unhealthy, but we need to keep in touch with possibility and hope. Frugality can be a precious commodity, one that can easily be lost to our disposable, "what's happening next, out with the old, in with the new" culture in which we are encouraged to set our sights on the newest and the brightest.

Try this approach on for size. Go out into the world and take a good, hard look at the familiar. Dig deeper. Maybe you'll find something you didn't know you had. When you can do that with objects, take it up a notch. Have a second look at the people around you. Look deeper in your heart, too. Maybe there's someone with whom you lost touch and can rekindle a friendship. Maybe there's someone you thought you didn't need to know because you assumed they had nothing to offer you. Well, before you figuratively toss them aside, try to see them as possibilities to uncover something marvellous, perhaps a side of them and you that you didn't "see" before now.

You think you know someone? Think again. Relationships are ripe with hope, so go ahead and take another glance. Remember, as long as there's possibility and hope, it's always worth a second look. You never know what goodness you may find. You know what I mean?

Learning to See

When I was a child, no one saw Bald Eagles. Oh, they could be seen in zoos or stuffed in some museums, but to see one in the wild, as part of everyday life, just didn't happen. In 1967, the species was listed as endangered, their numbers decimated by loss of habitat and reproductive impairment due to pesticides and heavy metals in the food chain. Even though I was interested in birds, I never used to look for Bald Eagles. Most of the remaining eagles were in Alaska, and to hope for a sighting in New Jersey was considered futile.

Thankfully, conservation measures have done a great deal for the eagles since that time, and on June 28, 2007, the Interior Department took the Bald Eagle off the Federal List of Endangered and Threatened Wildlife and Plants. Even though the numbers of these eagles have grown considerably since I was a child, it took some time before I spotted one. My expectations had to change. I had to learn how to see them.

My first eagle sighting in the wild was in 1992 while I was on a tour boat along the coast in Maine. Since then, I have viewed nesting pairs from a kayak in Maine, spotted them above reservoirs in New Jersey, and even viewed one soaring above my home. Not too long ago, I had my closest encounter to date. I had rounded the McCann Mill Road Bridge on my morning run with my dog Aztec. Heading up the dirt road in the lightly falling snow, I spotted, from a distance, a large bird in a tree, which, I presumed, would turn out to be a vulture. It wasn't. Something about it seemed odd to me because vultures usually group together, and this solitary bird was out over the water. It turned out to be a beautiful, mature Bald Eagle! It was content to sit there on its branch overlooking the Lamington River as we walked past it, actually getting within forty feet of it. I was spellbound, but the eagle was not spooked at all. Its gaze was fixed on us, having seen my dog and me, I'm certain, long before we saw it. Eventually, Aztec and I continued our run, leaving that magnificent bird to continue looking for fish in the swollen river. Cresting the rise in the road, I turned back one more time, and I saw the bird lift off from its perch and rise above the trees heading downstream. What a way to start the day!

I think, for many of us, we encounter God the way we might encounter eagles. There are lots of people who think God is on the endangered list, if He even exists at all. Some consider him to be extinct, categorizing any identification of God in the world as cases of misidentification. Sure, they've seen images of Him in churches, a broken, lifeless corpse suspended from a crucifix. Churches can be kind of like God museums where many go to catch a glimpse of the deity that's supposed to be the creator of the universe. Church is often the place where many people have been exposed to stories and movies about God and even confessed to a faith in him, but, sadly, that's where it often ends. Other than church, many people don't expect God to show up anywhere else in their lives. As a result, they don't look for him. They think the search is futile.

Well, here's the good news. God was never on the endangered list, and there are endless opportunities to see him. He blends in very well with his environment, so you need to know how to spot him, but once you know how to look, he'll be seen more and more often. Take a look and change your expectations because God is all around you. Look! God is in the stranger that holds the door for you in the elevator. God can be seen in the cancer ward wearing scrubs and holding the hands of the patients. God is there in the courage you feel inside of you when you confront the challenging times of your life. He's in the love and hugs you get from a family member. When you find yourself far from home, he's the breeze on your cheek that reminds you of the kisses from your children. He's there in every momentous sunset and sunrise of your life, and he's also beside you in the midst of your daily routine.

It doesn't matter where you are on your path of life. Take a moment and stop. Look around you. Do you see God? He's seen you since you were born. His gaze has been fixed on you during every step you've taken on your journey. He's there on His post over the river of life as much during your morning run as He is beside you on the commute to work. Look over your shoulder. God is and will forever be aloft, lifting off and soaring above and among us. We should be learning to see.

About the Author

Gordon Thomas Ward is a writer, presenter, and musician. Born in Tacoma, Washington, Mr. Ward's family moved to New Jersey when he was eleven months old. Both of his parents were talented artists and enjoyed the outdoors, and his family divided its time between the family's home in Bernardsville, New Jersey, and a summer cottage in Maine. After high school, Mr. Ward studied fine arts and psychology at Fairleigh Dickinson University in Madison, New Jersey, where his father was a professor. Gordon currently divides his professional time between writing and lecturing. He has worked as the Ministry Programs Director at a Presbyterian church, as a middle school and high school English and history teacher in the classroom, and as a group transformation facilitator in the experiential education field where he designed and facilitated teambuilding programs.

Clients have ranged from education groups in international conference settings to major corporations, government groups, athletic teams, schools, community groups, and individuals.

A lifelong writer, Mr. Ward's works have included books, speeches, newspaper and magazine articles, poetry, and a CD of original songs entitled *Welcome to the Past*. Gordon's earlier books include a book of original poetry entitled *Windows* (1994), *Life on the Shoulder: Rediscovery and Inspiration along the Lewis and Clark Trail* (Lucky Press 2005), *A Bit of Earth* (The History Press 2007), and *Ghosts of Central Jersey: Historic Haunts of the Somerset Hills* (The History Press 2008).

The author currently resides in northern New Jersey where he continually pursues his other passions for songwriting, natural history, and running.